Great Finishes:
Patterns & Techniques
for Quilting

BETTER HOMES AND GARDENS®

Great Finishes:
Patterns & Techniques
for Quilting

BETTER HOMES AND GARDENS® BOOKS

DES MOINES, IOWA

Better Homes and Gardens® Books, an imprint of Meredith® Books:
President, Book Group: Joseph J. Ward
Vice President, Editorial Director: Elizabeth P. Rice

Executive Editor: Maryanne Bannon
Senior Editor: Carol Spier
Assistant Editor: Bonita Eckhaus
Selections Editor: Eleanor Levie
Technical Editor: Cyndi Marsico
Technical Assistant: Diane Rode Schneck
Copy Editor: Mary Butler
Book Design: Beth Tondreau Design/M. Leo Albert, Daniel Rutter
Technical Artist: Phoebe Adams Gaughan
Photographer: Steven Mays
Photo Stylist: Susan Piatt
Production Manager: Bill Rose

The pattern for the quilt on page 66 can be found in the book *Quilter's Complete Guide*
by Marianne Fons and Liz Porter, Oxmoor House®, P.O. Box 2463, Birmingham,
Alabama 35282. The Flaming Pinwheel variation appears by permission of the authors
and publisher. For sashiko supplies, contact Quilters' Express to Japan,
80 East 11th Street, Suite 623, New York, New York 10003.

ISBN: 0-696-00084-9
Library of Congress Catalog Card Number: 93-080852

Printed in the United States of America
10 9 8 7 6 5 4 3 2 1

All of us at Better Homes and Gardens® Books are dedicated to offering you,
our customer, the best books we can create. We are particularly concerned that all
of our instructions for making projects are clear and accurate.
Please address your correspondence to Customer Service, Meredith® Press,
150 East 52nd Street, New York, NY 10022.

If you would like to order additional copies of any of our books,
call 1-800-678-2803 or check with your local bookstore.

Contents

This book is filled with ideas, patterns, and techniques for quilting—ideas that you can use wherever you wish. Quilting itself is not difficult, so we have not suggested a level of experience needed to use any of the ideas. Some quilting patterns require more time to set up than others, some require more time to stitch, and, of course, this time is relative to the size of your project. Have fun.

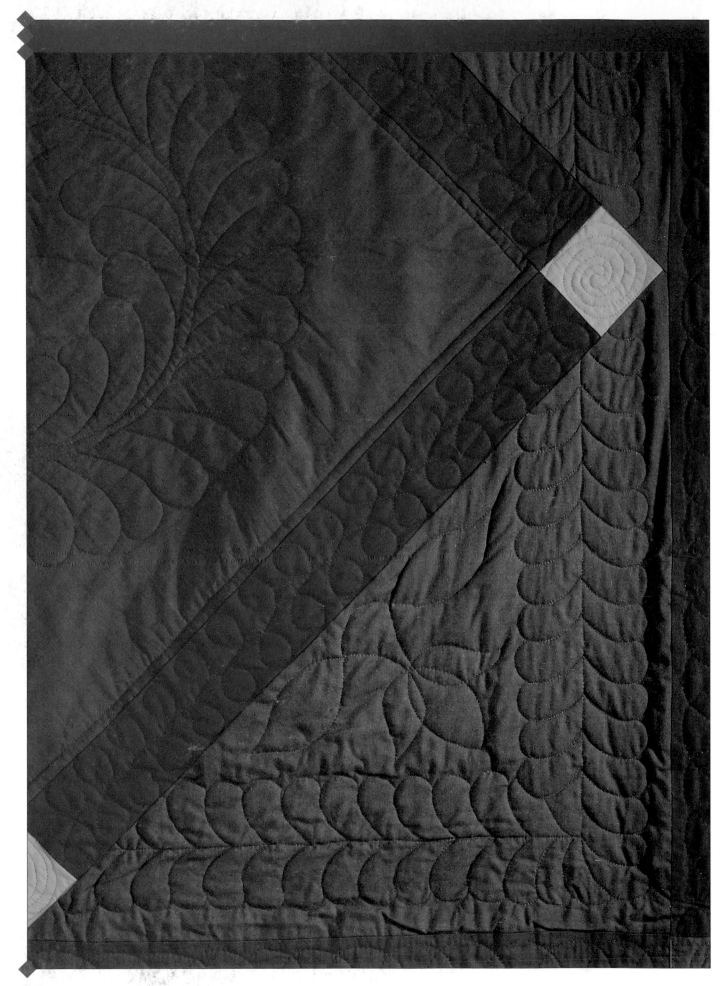

Color, fabric, patchwork, appliqué, borders, straight and diagonal sets—quilters' passions and enthusiasms brought together to make wonderful quilt tops—and then the moment of truth sets in…How to QUILT? By hand or machine? How much time to invest? Which motif? Traditional? Contemporary? Original? How dare they say "Quilt as desired"? Admit it, when you start a quilt you don't always give much thought to how you will quilt it. Sometimes you just don't want to make another decision, sometimes you know the quilt will tell you once it's assembled, sometimes you really haven't a clue even when you are looking at the completed top. So, how do you decide? How do other quilters know what to do? Where can you look for inspiration?

Start here. There are many wonderful ideas, shared by many terrific quilters. Some of the pieces you'll see were commissioned for this book, others we found at shows and through quilting friends. Some are presented as small samplers with complete directions, others are shown as large quilts with directions given for the quilting only. If you are a new quilter, try one of the samplers; if you are more experienced, transpose any of the ideas to your work. And be inspired— "Quilt as desired" should be fun, creative and satisfying.

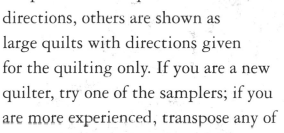

Apple Sampler

BY DIANE RODE SCHNECK

How do you know which type of batting is best for your quilt, or whether to quilt by hand or machine? Even experienced quilters with well-established preferences ask these questions from time to time, so we asked Diane to design a simple sampler that both beginners and pros could use to test materials and techniques. The left half of this small piece is filled with cotton batting, the right with low-loft polyester; the upper half is quilted by hand, the lower by machine. Follow our directions or adapt them to try out your own patterns.

Note: All dimensions except for binding are finished size.

BLOCK
4 blocks, 4″ square

BORDER
4 border strips, 2¼″ × 8″

CORNER SQUARE
Four 2¼″ corner squares

BINDING
1¼″-wide strip, pieced as
necessary and cut to size

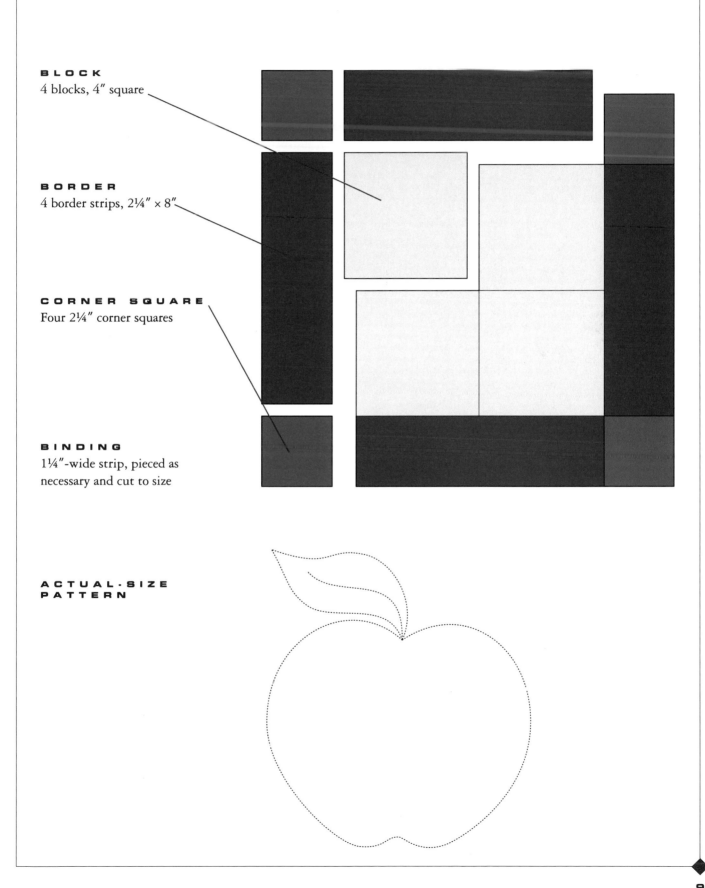

**ACTUAL-SIZE
PATTERN**

Yardages are based on 44″ fabric. Cut strips and patches following chart; see *Using the Cutting Charts*, page 88. Cut binding as directed below. All dimensions include ¼″ seam allowance and binding includes extra length. (NOTE: Angles on all patches are 90°.)

DIMENSIONS

FINISHED BLOCK
4″ square; about 5⅝″ diagonal

FINISHED QUILT
12½″ square

MATERIALS

MUSLIN SOLID
¼ yd.

RED PRINT
¼ yd.

DK. GREEN PRINT
¼ yd.

BINDING
Use remainder of fabric from blocks, cut and pieced, to make a 1¼″ × 60″ strip.

BACKING *
¾ yd.

BATTING *

THREAD

*Backing and batting should be cut and pieced as necessary so they are at least 4″ larger than quilt top on all sides, then trimmed to size after quilting.

	FIRST CUT		SECOND CUT	
Fabric and Yardage	Number of Pieces	Size	Number of Pieces	Size
BLOCKS				
Muslin Solid* ¼ yd.	1	4½″ × 20″	4	4½″ square
CORNER SQUARES				
Dk. Green Print ¼ yd.	1	2¾″ × 40″	4	2¾″ square
BORDER STRIPS				
Red Print ¼ yd.	2	2¾″ × 20″	4	2¾″ × 8½″
* Use remainder of fabric for cutting binding.				

Quilt Center

Arrange blocks in a 2 × 2 layout. Join pairs of blocks to make 2 rows. Join rows.

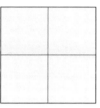

Border

Join corner squares to side border strips. Join border to quilt center, first plain strips at top and bottom, then pieced strips at sides.

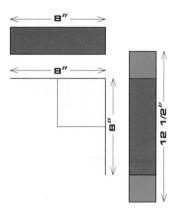

GREAT PATTERN TRACING TIP

If a source of illumination is placed behind a pattern and quilt top, the backlighting allows the design lines to show through to the front of the fabric for tracing. Prepare to trace a quilting pattern as follows:

♦ Sunny window: Tape the pattern to a clean, dry window on a sunny day. Tape the quilt top over the pattern.

♦ Light bulb: Open a separating table and place a clean, dry sheet of glass over the opening. Place a lamp (minus the shade) on the floor below the glass, and turn it on. Tape the pattern to the top of the glass. Secure the quilt top over the pattern with weights.

♦ Light box: Tape the pattern to the light box. Turn the light box on. Secure the quilt top over the pattern with weights.

Mark the design with a fine-point nonpermanent marker, experimenting first on scrap fabric to be sure your marker will make thin, light lines that can be removed after quilting.

Marking the Quilting Designs

Mark quilting designs on quilt top.

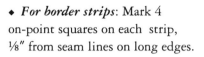

- *For quilt center*: Use actual-size pattern on page 9 to mark an apple on each block, centered.

- *For border strips*: Mark 4 on-point squares on each strip, ⅛″ from seam lines on long edges.

- *For corner squares*: Mark a square, ¼″ from seams.

Assembling the Quilt Layers

Prepare batting and backing. Assemble quilt layers.

TO TEST THE EFFECT OF YOUR QUILTING

If you want to make a sampler to test the effects on two different types of batting (e.g., cotton vs. polyester; thick vs. thin), stitch together the two types, side by side with long herringbone stitches as shown, and cut the resulting piece so that the seam will be along the horizontal or vertical center of the quilt.

You can also test the effects of quilting by hand and by machine on both types of batting as we did by quilting half of your project with each method. If the batting seam is along the vertical center of the quilt, quilt the top and bottom halves differently to get four different effects: (1) hand-quilting on thin batting; (2) hand-quilting on thick batting; (3) machine-quilting on thin batting; and (4) machine-quilting on thick batting. If the batting seam is along the horizontal center, quilt the left and right halves differently to get the four sample effects.

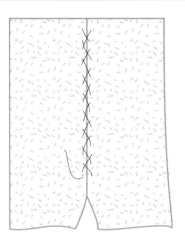

Quilting the Designs

Quilt on all marked lines; see the *Great Quilting Tip*, below.

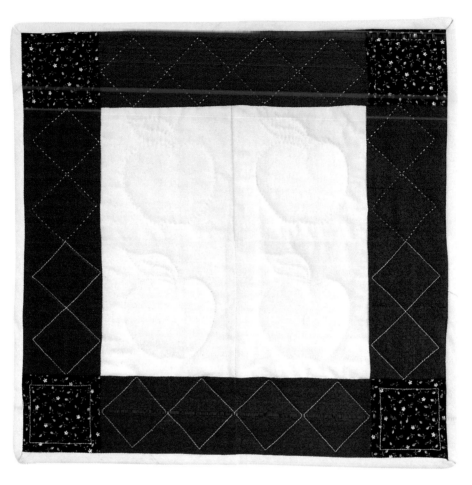

Trim batting and backing to ⅜" beyond outermost seam line. Bind quilt edges.

GREAT QUILTING TIP

Whether you quilt your sampler by hand or by machine, you can stitch the design on each border strip in a continuous route.

Begin at one end of the design (A) to stitch the most direct path to the opposite end (B). Without breaking the thread, continue stitching back to A.

A   B

Baker's Basics Sampler

BY KATHARINE BRAINARD

Out of ideas for quilting motifs? Can't find a template the right size? Don't want to enlarge or reduce on a copy machine? It could be that the perfect template awaits discovery close at hand. Katharine used cookie cutters, a miniature tart pan and small scissors to create the designs for this lighthearted sampler. She quilted it by machine, stitching with the feed dogs both up and down—even using a free-motion zigzag stitch inside the flowers. Make the sampler as shown, or use everyday objects to "quilt as desired."

Note: All dimensions except for binding are finished size.

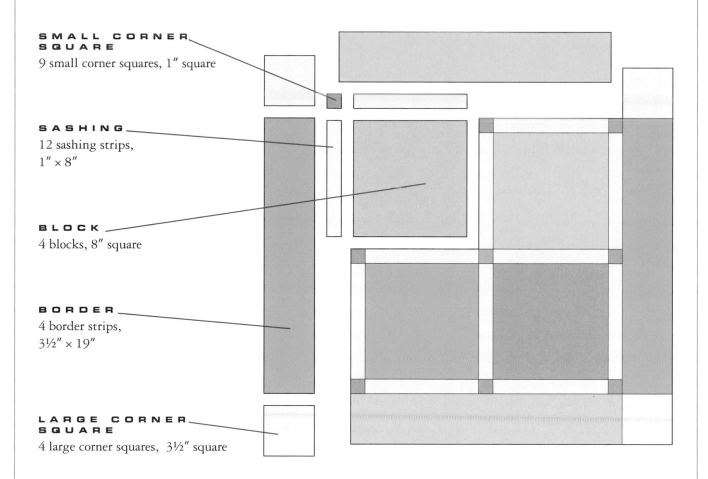

SMALL CORNER SQUARE

9 small corner squares, 1″ square

SASHING

12 sashing strips, 1″ × 8″

BLOCK

4 blocks, 8″ square

BORDER

4 border strips, 3½″ × 19″

LARGE CORNER SQUARE

4 large corner squares, 3½″ square

BINDING

1″-wide strip, pieced as necessary and cut to size

Yardages are based on 44" fabric. Cut strips and patches following charts; see *Using the Cutting Charts*, page 88. Cut binding as directed below. All dimensions include ¼" seam allowance and binding includes extra length. (NOTE: Angles on all patches are 90°.)

DIMENSIONS

FINISHED BLOCK
8" square; about 11⅜" diagonal

FINISHED QUILT
26" square

MATERIALS

LT. YELLOW SOLID
½ yd.

PINK SOLID
½ yd.

LAVENDER SOLID
½ yd.

LT. BLUE SOLID
½ yd.

GREEN SOLID
½ yd.

BINDING
½ yd. plaid is cut and pieced to make a 1" × 120" bias strip.

BACKING*
1 yd.

BATTING*

THREAD

*Backing and batting should be cut and pieced as necessary so they are at least 4" larger than quilt top on all sides, then trimmed to size after quilting.

GREAT TEMPLATE TIP

Try using cookie cutters and other everyday items as sturdy, reusable templates for simple quilting motifs. If you look around your home and office, you are sure to find inspiration: serving and eating utensils, pots, trivets, scissors, French curves, tape dispensers, baby shoes, barrettes, a change purse, a miniature steam iron, or even your hand! As long as it has at least one flat, stable surface for tracing around, almost anything can be used as a template.

Mark individual shapes directly onto your fabric, or make a pattern for complex groupings. Quilt the marked outline(s), then stitch additional outlines 1/4" to 1/2" apart, either inside or outside the shapes, for double-outline or echo quilting.

FIRST CUT			SECOND CUT				
			Number of Pieces				
Fabric and Yardage	Number of Pieces	Size	For Blocks	For Sashing Strips	For Small Corner Squares	For Large Corner Squares	Size
Lt. Yellow Solid ½ yd.	3	1½" × 40"	—	12	—	—	1½" × 8½"
	1	4" × 20"	—	—	—	4	4" square
Pink Solid ½ yd.	1	1½" × 20"	—	—	8	—	1½" square
	—	—	1	—	—	—	8½" square
Lavender Solid ½ yd.	—	—	1	—	—	—	8½" square

FIRST CUT			SECOND CUT			
			Number of Pieces			
Fabric and Yardage	Number of Pieces	Size	For Blocks	For Small Corner Squares	For Border Strips	Size
Lt. Blue Solid ½ yd.	1	4" × 40"	—	—	2	4" × 19½"
	—	—	1	—	—	8½" square
Green Solid ½ yd.	1	4" × 40"	—	—	2	4" × 19½"
	—	—	1	—	—	8½" square
	—	—	—	1	—	1½" square

Quilt Center

Arrange units as shown. Join units to make rows. Join rows.

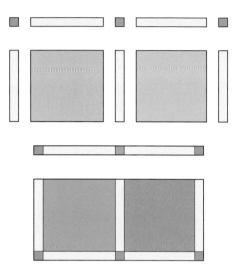

Border

Join large corner squares to side border strips. Join border to quilt center, first plain strips at top and bottom, then pieced strips at sides.

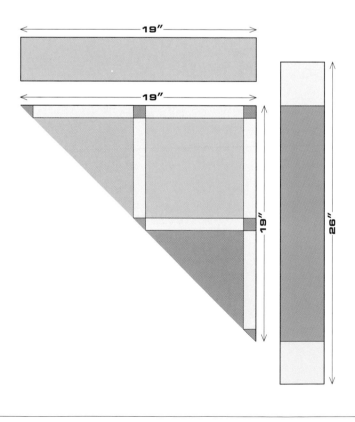

Creating the Quilting Designs

Mark quilting designs on quilt top following directions below, or use designs of your own choice; see the *Great Template Tip* on page 16. Trace shapes directly onto fabric, or make a pattern for each area of design.

♦ *For lavender block:* Use 3″-high gingerbread man and woman, 1¾″-high star, and 1⅛″-high heart. Mark star at center of block. Mark left half of design on block, then rotate as shown to mark right half; do not repeat star.

♦ *For green block:* Use 3″-diameter scalloped-edge circle (we used a small tart pan) and a 2½″-diameter smooth-edge circle (the removable bottom of the pan). Mark left half of design on block, making ¼″ wide stems, 2″ and 4½″ high; and 1¾″ long leaves, ¾″ and 1″ wide. Flop design as shown to mark right half of block.

♦ *For blue block:* Use hearts 2⅝″, 1⅞″, and 1⅛″ high. Mark design on each quarter of block, rotating as shown.

♦ *For pink block:* Use 3¾″-high scissors and 1⅛″-high heart. Mark heart at center of block. Mark scissors on each quarter of block, rotating as shown.

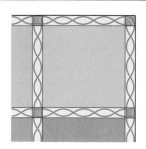

♦ **For sashing and small corner squares:** Use ¾" × 2" single-line cable template, or draft cable using a portion of a 3"-diameter lid or saucer. Mark 3 complete cables and 2 half-cables on each sashing strip, centered between long edges. Connect half-cables by marking straight lines across all squares except those at outer corners; mark symmetrical corners on unmarked squares.

♦ **For large corner squares:** Use stars from lavender block and green border strips. Mark concentric stars on each large corner square, centered.

♦ **For blue border strips:** Use hearts from blue block. Mark 7 trios of concentric hearts, equally spaced, across each strip, alternating right-side up and upside down trios.

♦ **For green border strips:** Use 2⅝"-high star. Arrange 7 stars on each strip in same manner as for heart trios on blue border strips.

Assembling the Quilt Layers

Prepare batting and backing. Assemble quilt layers.

Quilting the Designs

Machine-quilt on all marked lines. Fill flower centers with stippling or an allover design of your choice. Fill in around stars on green border strips with closely spaced stippling loops; see *Machine-Stippling* on page 43.

Trim batting and backing even with quilt top. Bind quilt edges.

Pansy Block

BY DIANE RODE SCHNECK

A ll quilters encounter moments when conventional quilting templates just don't seem to complement the quilt in progress. One way to be sure your quilting harmonizes with your quilt is to borrow the motifs printed on the fabric and adapt, enlarge, and rearrange them to suit. Here, pansies taken from an allover print fill a plain block. Getting the right effect takes a bit of trial and error, but you can adapt almost any print (you'll find a photocopier very helpful). Quilt complex motifs by hand or free-motion on the machine.

Note: All dimensions except for binding are finished size.

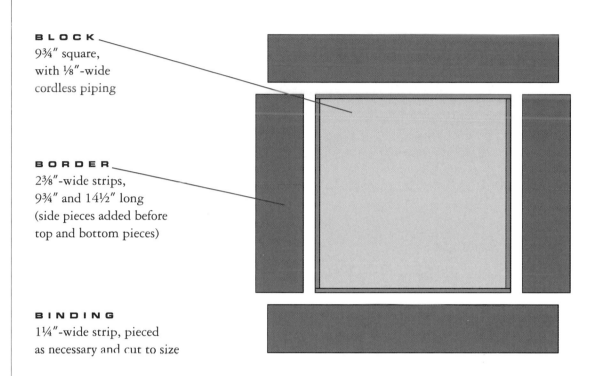

BLOCK
9¾″ square,
with ⅛″-wide
cordless piping

BORDER
2⅜″-wide strips,
9¾″ and 14½″ long
(side pieces added before
top and bottom pieces)

BINDING
1¼″-wide strip, pieced
as necessary and cut to size

GREAT DESIGN IDEA

If you increase the finished size of the Pansy block and/or the border, you can make a 16″-square pillow. Use any combination of dimensions that will result in a 16″ square; see the examples below. If you enlarge the block, you may want to also enlarge the quilting motifs that will be stitched on it; see Adapting Fabric Motifs, page 25.

16″-square pillow = 10″-square block + 3″-wide border
16″-square pillow = 11″-square block + 2 1/2″-wide border
16″-square pillow = 12″-square block + 2″-wide border

To make a pillow, stitch together the quilt top, assemble the layers, and quilt a design on the block. Add a pillow back and insert a 16″-square knife-edge pillow form.

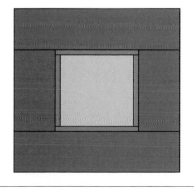
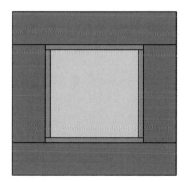
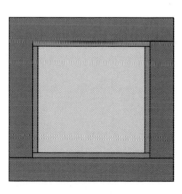

Yardages are based on 44″ fabric. Cut strips and patches following chart; see *Using the Cutting Charts*, page 88. Cut binding as directed below. All dimensions include ¼″ seam allowance and binding includes extra length. (NOTE: Angles on all patches are 90°.)

DIMENSIONS

FINISHED BLOCK
9¾″ square; about 13¾″ diagonal

FINISHED QUILT
14½″ square

MATERIALS

PINK SOLID
½ yd.

PLUM SOLID
¼ yd.

PINK/RED/PURPLE PRINT
¼ yd.

BINDING
Use ¼ yd. plum solid, cut and pieced, to make a 1¼″ × 70″ strip. Reserve remainder of fabric to cut piping.

BACKING*
¾ yd.

BATTING*

THREAD

*Backing and batting should be cut and pieced as necessary so they are at least 4″ larger than quilt top on all sides, then trimmed to size after quilting.

FIRST CUT			SECOND CUT	
Fabric and Yardage	Number of Pieces	Size	Number of Pieces	Size
BLOCK				
Pink Solid ½ yd.	1	9¾″ square		
PIPING				
Plum Solid*	1	¾″ × 40″	4	¾″ × 9¾″
BORDER				
Pink/Red/Purple Print ¼ yd.	2	2⅞″ × 40″	2	2⅞″ × 10¼″
			2	2⅞″ × 9¾″
* Use remainder of fabric from binding.				

Print fabrics are a wonderful resource for flowers and other designs that can be adapted for quilting motifs. Diane Schneck created a stylized enlargement of several flowers in the border fabric of her Pansy Block wallhanging for the quilting motif, giving her project a unified look. You can copy the actual-size patterns for her quilting motifs, below, or adapt prints from the fabric in your quilt as follows.

Place a sheet of tracing paper or acetate over the print fabric and trace individual shapes or a group of shapes, eliminating tiny details and modifying or simplifying the design. After removing the tracing, make any adjustments to it, such as regularizing, overlapping, duplicating, flopping, or rearranging the shapes, to form a pleasing pattern. You can complete any partial shapes that are printed "behind" others on the fabric, as Diane did to create the patterns for individual flowers and leaves. You could also add new shapes, such as stems or branches. Let your creativity guide your adaptation.

When you are satisfied with your pattern, enlarge or reduce it to fit your project. Transfer the quilting pattern to the quilt top as you would any other pattern.

PATTERNS

ACTUAL-SIZE PATTERNS

**ACTUAL·SIZE
PATTERNS**

Piping

Baste piping strips to quilt block, first at sides, then at top and bottom; see the *Great Piping Idea* on page 29.

Border

Join border to quilt center, first shorter strips at sides, then longer strips at top and bottom; stitches will also permanently secure piping.

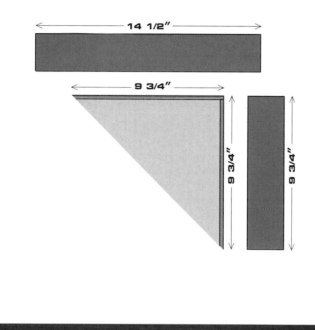

Marking the Quilting Design

Mark quilting design on block for motif quilting, using actual-size patterns on pages 25 and 26 or patterns of your own choice; see *Adapting Fabric Motifs* on page 25.

Assembling the Quilt Layers

Prepare batting and backing. Assemble quilt layers.

Quilting the Designs

Hand-quilt on all marked lines, using matching or contrasting thread.

Trim batting and backing to ⅜″ beyond outermost seam line. Bind quilt edges.

Cordless piping can be used to accent individual components of a quilt the same way a mat sets off a framed picture. Solid or print piping that contrasts with adjacent fabrics on the quilt top gives the maximum effect.

Because piping is applied on top of a component, the finished size of the underneath piece remains the same, but the visible area is reduced by the finished width of the piping. For example, the finished Pansy Block is 9 3/4" square and the finished size of the piping is 1/8", leaving a visible block size of 9 1/2" square. Experiment (on graph paper first, if you desire) with the effects that can be achieved with various color combinations and placement of piping to add a new look to your quilting projects.

The cut length of a piping strip should be the same as the edge of the quilt component to which it will be attached. If you want the finished size of your piping to be slightly narrower or wider than the 1/8" finished width of the piping on the Pansy Block wallhanging, use the following equation to determine the cut width of your strips:

PIPING STRIP WIDTH = (2 x FINISHED WIDTH) + 1/2"

To prepare piping, press the strips in half lengthwise, right side out. To apply piping, baste each strip to the component piece with the folded edge toward the center and the raw edges aligned. The piping will be joined permanently as additional components are stitched to the piped edges.

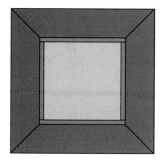
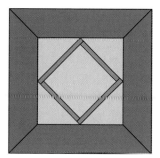
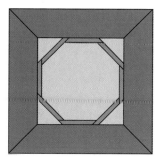

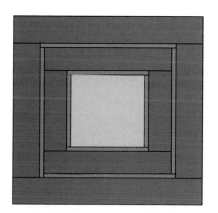
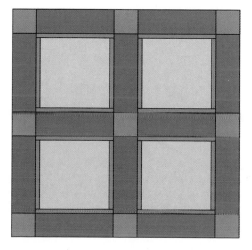

Wild Animals Appliqué

BY KATHARINE BRAINARD

Katharine Brainard often makes whimsical quilts for children. Each block of this quilt was pieced to represent ground and sky, and then machine-appliquéd with an animal and other details—all drawn freehand. Once Katharine had the quilt top assembled, she drew additional motifs such as puffy clouds, moon and stars, and a setting sun, quilting them by machine to complete each scene. She also quilted in-the-ditch along sashing strips and the outline of each appliqué.

Creating the Quilting Designs

If you want to use quilting to complete a picture, choose simple motifs that can be recognized by their outlines. If you plan to quilt by machine, try to pick motifs that can be stitched in one continuous line so that you will not have to cut and tie off any more thread ends than absolutely necessary. If you are timid, plan your design on tracing paper placed over your appliqué. Otherwise draw directly onto the fabric with a non-permanent marker.

Here are some other motifs you might consider:

BIRDS IN FLIGHT

WIND OR FLOWING WATER

FALLEN LEAVES

BRICKS OR STONES ON A PATH OR WALL

RIPPLES ON A POND

FLOWERS IN A MEADOW

WAVES

Jungle Moonlight

BY DIANE RODE SCHNECK

Diane Rode Schneck refers to this stunning string quilt as "My Save-the-Earth quilt." She used dozens of green-hued cotton prints and a few metallics to make diagonally striped blocks. The lightest hues are set off-center like a shaft of sunlight striking through a canopy of leaves. This piece is hand-quilted with hundreds of randomly placed small leaf shapes. Crystal beads and rhinestones scattered over the surface complete the sensation of filtering light.

Creating the Quilting Design

Some of the leaf shapes Diane used as quilting motifs are based on the prints of the fabrics, others come from her imagination or memory. They are all small—no more than two or three inches long or wide. She drew them freehand on the quilt top, tilting and overlapping them with no reference to the piecing, so that the surface is almost completely covered.

The quilting of this wallhanging reiterates its leafy green theme. It was more important to Diane to create a feeling of lushness and abundance than to showcase the quilting motifs, and the overall effect is subtle—a wonderful secret to discover on a close viewing.

GREAT MOTIF TIP

Be sure to consider scale and proportion when choosing a thematic quilting motif. If you want to create a dense allover pattern, pick a simple motif—note that most of Diane's leaves have only three lobes and just a few veins—otherwise the theme will be difficult to distinguish. If your pattern will be larger or more widely spaced, you can use more complex motifs. The busier your fabric or patchwork is, the more subtle the quilted motif will be.

Mood Indigo

BY LINDA MASON

Sashiko is a traditional Japanese stitching technique that features natural motifs. Many of the patterns connote gender or class, or are symbolic of character traits. Most sashiko patterns can be repeated to create allover designs. They are often worked on solid (and not necessarily pieced) indigo fabric, creating an effect of complex woven or printed cloth. The thread used is heavier than for conventional Western quilting, and can be worked on one or two layers of fabric, batting is optional.

Drafting the Patterns

Linda Mason made her 23½″ × 29″ kimono wallhanging from four basic units: the plain collar and body, and the pieced right sleeve and bottom left corner. The right sleeve is made of 3¾″-long arrows. The arcs on the bottom left corner unit can be drawn with a compass or circle template, using the same circle to mark all of the arcs.

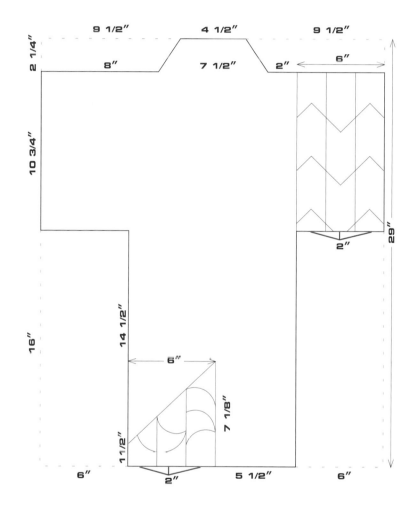

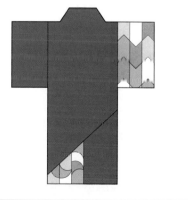

Marking the Sashiko Designs

Sashiko designs are traditionally drafted directly on fabric, but we have provided actual-size patterns (on pages 38 and 39) that you can use.

On the kimono the Butterfly Crest medallion is centered on the body, about 5¼″ from the top edge. The Chrysanthemum sits sideways on the body along the inner edge of the left sleeve, about 1¼″ from the top. The Cypress Fence is used as the background for the body, with the design lines positioned on the bias. The bottom boundary of the Cypress Fence is a row of Bush Clover, with Maple Leaves and angular lines of Pine Bark adorning the bottom right corner. Flowing Water is marked twice on the left sleeve, the outer motif slightly offset to be a reflection of the inner one.

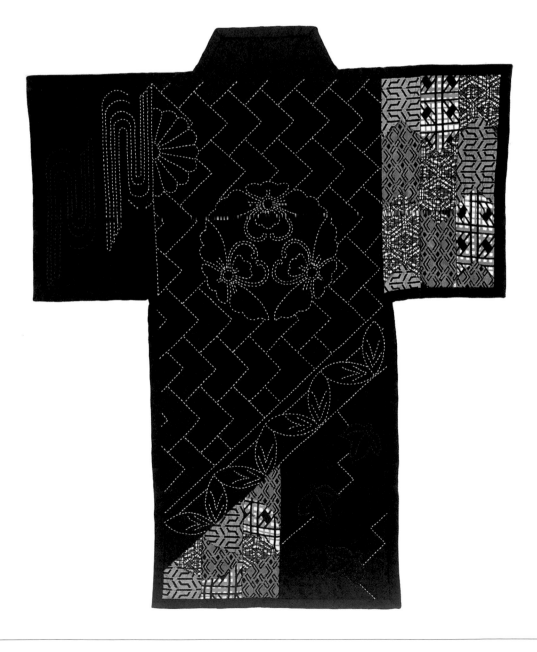

Quilting the Designs

Sashiko is a running stitch, 5 to 7 stitches-per-inch instead of the standard 10 to 12 stitches-per-inch of conventional hand-quilting. Sashiko is worked so the stitches and the spaces between them are of equal length; see the *Great Planning Tip*, below. It can be done on a single layer of fabric (embroidery) or, as for the kimono wallhanging, through the assembled layers of a quilt (quilting).

Linda Mason quilted the solid areas of the kimono in sashiko, using white for most of the motifs and background, and red for the maple leaves and reflected water ripples. On the pieced units she did conventional hand-quilting in-the-ditch around each patch.

GREAT PLANNING TIP

The beauty of sashiko is in the characteristic evenness and precision in the placement of the stitches against a highly contrasting background. Careful planning is the key to ensuring the same number of identical stitches and spaces between pairs of similar points on the design.

Before beginning to stitch, study each section of each motif to identify the different shapes and lengths of individual design lines. Also note intersections where design lines meet or cross because, as a rule, the stitches should never touch each other but end equidistant from the intersection. If it seems necessary to adjust the stitch length (and spacing) along a design line, the adjustment should be made uniformly to the entire line of stitching.

ACTUAL-SIZE
PATTERNS

CHRYSANTHEMUM
(KIKU)

CYPRESS FENCE
(HIGAKI)

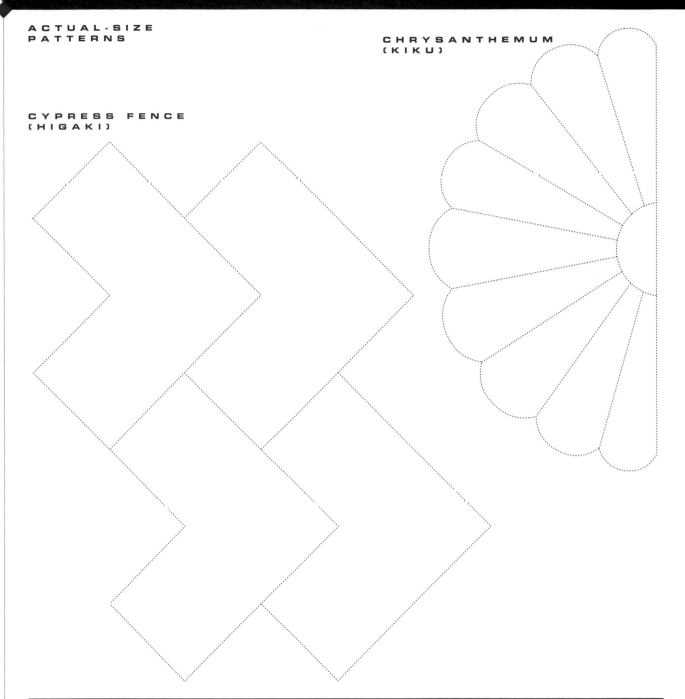

GREAT FABRIC AND THREAD TIP

Traditional sashiko is done on 100%-cotton fabric (noncolorfast indigo) with special 100%-cotton thread, but you can use broadcloth or tightly woven cotton-polyester blends and any of the following types of cotton embroidery thread for beautiful results:

THREAD	WORK WITH
Embroidery floss, 6-ply	4 to 6 strands
Pearl cotton, #5 or #8	2 strands
Candlewicking yarn, 4-ply	2 to 4 strands

FLOWING WATER
(KANZEMIZU)

BUTTERFLY CREST
(CHO)

MAPLE
LEAF

BUSH CLOVER
(HAGI)

Forest Floor

BY SONYA LEE BARRINGTON

California quilter Sonya Lee Barrington has made a series of quilts interpreting the contrast of light, shadow and color on a forest floor. She uses simple geometric pieces in solid and subtly patterned fabrics, with hand-quilting that sometimes parallels the seams and sometimes loops in freehand curves between them. Here, to carry the dappled effect of the center onto the plain border, Sonya inserted prairie points, then used variously spaced small stitches to create a texture that both absorbs and reflects light.

Sonya's hand-stippling technique creates a scrunched texture that has more depth than machine-stippling, which tends to compress the batting. Note how the texture varies, as your eye moves around the borders between groups of stitches that are spaced closer together and further apart.

Hand-stippling is a very easy technique that requires no marking (although you may want to designate certain areas to be more densely stitched than others) and you may find it relaxing to place the intentionally irregular stitches. To prepare, layer and baste the quilt layers in the same manner as for conventional quilting. Thread your needle and bring it through to the top of the quilt, burying the knot between the layers.

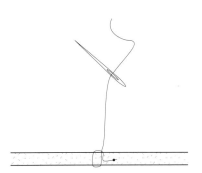 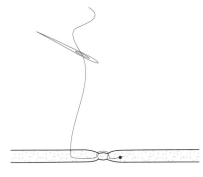 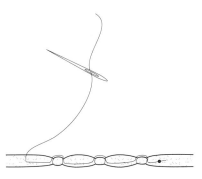

1. Make one very small stitch through all layers, passing the needle to the back of the quilt, then bringing it to the top again where it first emerged.

2. Reinsert the needle through the top layer into the batting, then slide it through to where you want the next stitch to be; bring the needle to the top again.

3. Repeat steps 1 and 2 to stipple the area. Space the stitches from ½″ to 2″ apart, or as necessary to achieve the effect you want. Note that for each stitch there are two bars of thread on the top and one on the back of the quilt.

GREAT QUILTING THREAD TIP

The thread you choose can alter the effect of your quilting. Note how Sonya used metallic thread for the loopy lines quilted over the patchwork of Forest Floor—it enhances the movement and adds sparkle to her hand-dyed and marbled fabrics. Diane Schneck also chose metallic thread for the curves on her blue and black Night Quilt; see page 62. Clear monofilament adds a subtle sheen; see the Diamond-in-a-Square quilt on page 46. If you stitch with contrasting pearl cotton, your quilting will double as embroidery; see the pillow on page 80.

Traditionally, stippling is used as a filler. It can take the form of straight, regularly spaced rows of stitches (lined up or staggered), or of random zigzags, curves, or loops. Stippling should be done with closely spaced lines of stitching, from ¼" to ½" apart, which will give a low-relief design area with a textured appearance. Note the stippled background of the star borders on the Baker's Basics Sampler on pages 14 and 21.

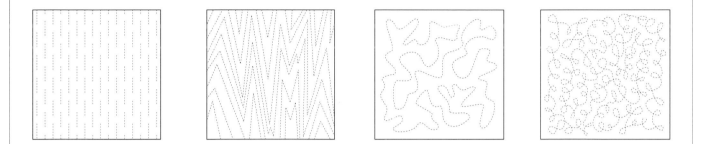

Machine-Stippling

Place your quilt in a hoop (one that will fit easily under the needle of your sewing machine) to keep the layers smooth and taut. Reposition the hoop during quilting as necessary.

Use a darning or embroidery foot, and either lower or cover the feed dogs so that you have complete control over the movement of the quilt through the machine. There is no need to adjust the stitch length. Control the needle speed with the motor-control pedal as usual, and guide the fabric in the desired pattern with your hands.

Always make a sample to test the effect, using the fabric and batting in your project: Your quilting lines should look smooth and even on both the front and back; adjust the tension on the threads in the machine as necessary. If you are new to machine-stippling, you might want to practice on a small piece such as a potholder.

> **GREAT STIPPLING TIP**
>
> If you are timid about stitching random freehand patterns, purchase a stippling template and mark your quilt top in the conventional manner.

Diamond-in-a-Square

BY ANN BOYCE
QUILTED BY JEANNE ELLIOTT

Ann Boyce is known for her exuberant and not necessarily traditional quilts and wearables. She grew up in Pennsylvania and made this quilt, which reflects her love of Amish designs, "for my bed." It is machine quilted, with clear monofilament in the needle and black thread in the bobbin. The traditional motifs are readily available on templates. By planning her quilting routes carefully, Jeanne Elliott was able to stitch each of them in a continuous line.

*Note: All dimensions are finished size.
The finished quilt is about 75" square.*

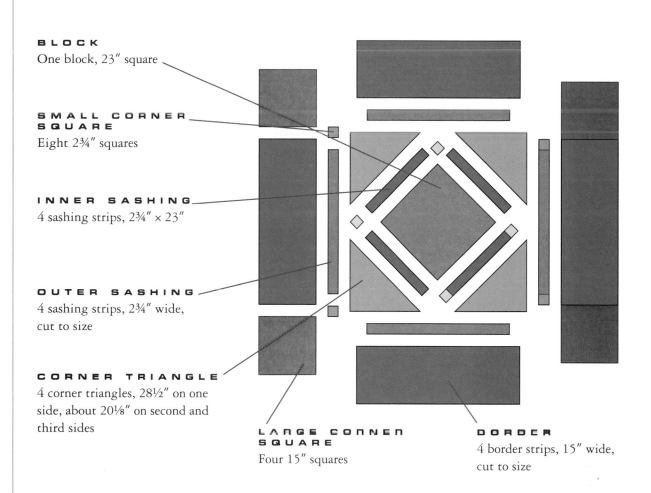

BLOCK
One block, 23" square

SMALL CORNER SQUARE
Eight 2¾" squares

INNER SASHING
4 sashing strips, 2¾" × 23"

OUTER SASHING
4 sashing strips, 2¾" wide,
cut to size

CORNER TRIANGLE
4 corner triangles, 28½" on one
side, about 20⅛" on second and
third sides

LARGE CORNER SQUARE
Four 15" squares

BORDER
4 border strips, 15" wide,
cut to size

GREAT DRAFTING TIP

The diamond-in-a-square pattern can be scaled to almost any size you wish, using the drafting method below to keep the components proportional.

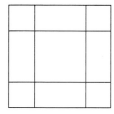 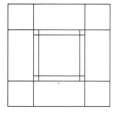 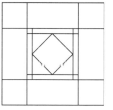 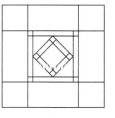

1. On graph paper mark the square outline of your quilt. Draw a border inside the square, about 1/4 the width of the quilt.
2. Add sashing, about 1/5 the width of the border.
3. Connect the centers of the sashing strips to form a diamond.
4. Add sashing inside the diamond the same width as the outer sashing.

Marking the Quilting Designs

Using purchased templates can speed up the marking of even the largest of quilts. Templates are available in quilting shops and by mail for a wide range of quilting motifs in a variety of sizes, which can in turn be reduced or enlarged to fit any project.

Ann Boyce used purchased feather, curl, cable, and flower templates on most of the quilt components, then added a hand-drawn double-outline spiral on each small corner square; see the actual-size pattern, opposite, which you can resize as desired.

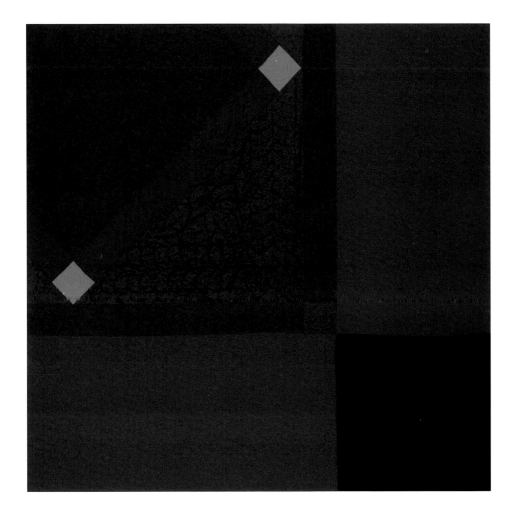

GREAT PLANNING TIP

To help you visualize the best route along your quilting motif, place tracing paper over the pattern or template. Draw over the design, trying to complete it in one continuous line, or as few lines as possible. Use arrows, numbers, or different color pencils to help you find the best route for a complex motif. If necessary, adapt the motif by connecting or smoothing some of the design lines. If you are unsure of the workability of your plan, test-stitch the route on a scrap of fabric.

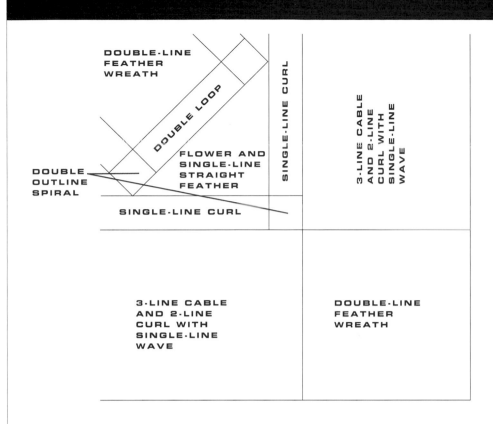

DOUBLE-LINE
FEATHER
WREATH

DOUBLE LOOP

SINGLE-LINE CURL

3-LINE CABLE
AND 2-LINE
CURL WITH
SINGLE-LINE
WAVE

DOUBLE
OUTLINE
SPIRAL

FLOWER AND
SINGLE-LINE
STRAIGHT
FEATHER

SINGLE-LINE CURL

3-LINE CABLE
AND 2-LINE
CURL WITH
SINGLE-LINE
WAVE

DOUBLE-LINE
FEATHER
WREATH

ACTUAL-SIZE PATTERN:
DOUBLE OUTLINE SPIRAL

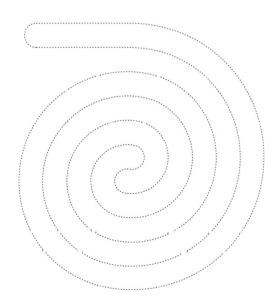

GREAT CABLE TIP

If you need to shorten or lengthen a cable design to fit your border, make adjustments at the center of the repeats (where they are the tallest) rather than at the ends, and connect all lines smoothly. Altering the length of a repeat may also affect its height.

You can adjust one or more cables on any number of border sides as needed. The least noticeable locations are generally the center and ends of each border side. If you find that you are adjusting a lot of cables on your quilt, you might try using a different size template.

Planning a Route

The quilting on any project can go more quickly if the designs are stitched along the most continuous paths possible. When quilting by hand, you can slide your needle through the batting to bridge any breaks between design lines or to avoid retracing an already stitched line. When quilting by machine, you do not have that option, so it is even more important to plan the best route along a design before you begin to sew.

On the Diamond-in-a-Square quilt, the single-line curl, double-outline spiral, double loop and flower were each stitched with one uninterrupted line of stitching. The 3-line cable and 2-line curl with the single-line wave were stitched with one continuous line of stitching for each design line. For each feather pattern, some parts of the design were stitched twice so that the line of stitching did not have to be broken.

◆ *For the Double-Line Feather Wreath:* If necessary, adjust the motif so that each ring of feathers sits on a smooth circular line. First, stitch the inner and outer circular lines. Then, begin stitching one feather where it intersects the base circle; stitch around it until you reach the base again; pivot, and repeat to stitch the adjacent feather. Repeat around each ring of feathers.

◆ *For the Single-Line Straight Feather:* First, stitch the straight line along the center of the motif. Then, begin stitching one feather where it intersects the straight line; stitch around it until you reach the line again; pivot, and repeat to stitch the adjacent feather on the same side of the line. Repeat along each side of the line.

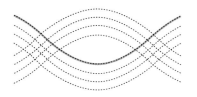

◆ *For a multi-line cable, curl or wave:* Stitch the entire length of each line of the motif in one continuous line.

◆ *For the Flower:* Begin stitching in the middle of the motif, at the base of the petals. Work in the direction of the arrows to stitch the left leaf, the right leaf, the left petal, the middle petal and then the right petal.

GREAT DRAFTING TIP

Drawing spirals may seem like a daunting task, but with a pencil, ruler, and either a compass or templates, you can draft a perfect spiral using a straight line, dots, a circle, and some semicircles.

Drafting methods are shown below for simple single- and double-line spirals drawn from the outside inward; you can reverse the order in which the semicircles are drawn if you prefer to create your spirals from the center outward. For the single-line spiral, the number of equidistant dots along the center guideline can be either even or odd. The double-line spiral requires an odd number of equidistant dots to make the pattern work out correctly.

Draw your spirals at a convenient size, then resize and/or flop them to suit your project.

SINGLE-LINE SPIRAL STEP 1 STEP 2 STEP 3 STEP 4
STEP 5 STEP 6 STEP 7 STEP 8

DOUBLE-LINE SPIRAL STEP 1 STEP 2 STEP 3 STEP 4
STEP 5 STEP 6

Sunflowers Appliqué

BY POLLY WHITEHORN

I f you enjoy doing appliqué you have no doubt considered how best to quilt the background areas. Of course, you can use a simple allover grid, breaking the stitching at the edges of the appliqués, but when you want something with a bit more punch, try echo quilting to emphasize your design. Award-winning quilter Polly Whitehorn specializes in both traditional and whimsical appliqué, so we asked her to design a small piece that would demonstrate the versatility of echo quilting—and be fun to make and display.

Note: All dimensions except for binding are finished size.

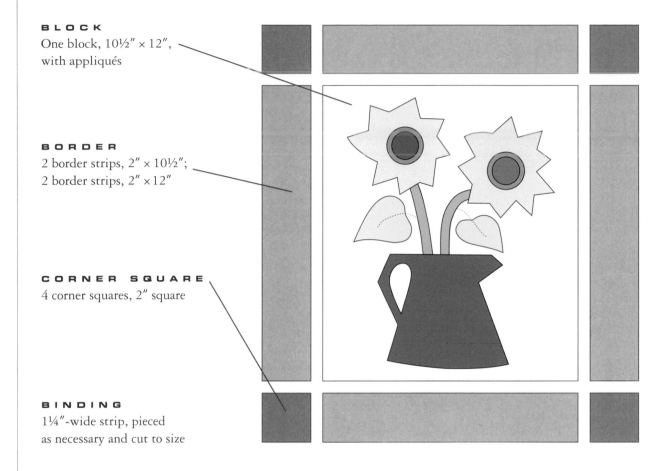

BLOCK
One block, 10½″ × 12″, with appliqués

BORDER
2 border strips, 2″ × 10½″;
2 border strips, 2″ × 12″

CORNER SQUARE
4 corner squares, 2″ square

BINDING
1¼″-wide strip, pieced as necessary and cut to size

GREAT MARKING TIP

You can establish straight guidelines for single-outline, double-outline, echo, or diagonal quilting without actually putting marks on the fabric: Use drafting, masking, or quilting tape that is 1/4″ wide or whatever width best suits your project. Place a strip of tape on the quilt to establish one line (or a pair of parallel lines) at a time, moving it as needed. Tape can leave a residue on fabric, so do not leave it on your quilt for any length of time.

Yardages are based on 44″ fabric. Use actual-size patterns on page 57 to prepare templates #1 to #7 for hand-appliqué. Cut strips, patches, and appliqués following charts; see *Using the Cutting Charts*, page 88. Cut binding as directed below. All dimensions include ¼″ seam allowance and binding includes extra length. (NOTE: Angles on all patches are 90°.)

DIMENSIONS

FINISHED BLOCK
10½″ × 12″

FINISHED QUILT
14½″ × 16″

MATERIALS

☐ **WHITE SOLID**
½ yd.

▢ **MED. YELLOW PRINT**
¼ yd.

▢ **DK. YELLOW PRINT**
¼ yd.

▢ **LT. YELLOW/ RED PRINT**
¼ yd.

▢ **MED. BROWN/ YELLOW PRINT**
¼ yd.

▢ **DK. BROWN/ YELLOW PRINT**
¼ yd.

▢ **LT. GREEN PRINT**
¼ yd.

▢ **DK. GREEN PRINT**
¼ yd.

▢ **BLUE/BLACK STRIPE**
¼ yd.

▢ **BLACK/WHITE CHECK**
¼ yd.

▣ **BLACK PRINT**
¼ yd.

BINDING
¼ yd. black solid is cut and pieced to make a 1¼″ × 70″ strip.

BACKING *
¾ yd.

BATTING *

THREAD

EMBROIDERY FLOSS
One skein each lt. green and lt. olive

*Backing and batting should be cut and pieced as necessary so they are at least 4″ larger than quilt top on all sides, then trimmed to size after quilting.

GREAT FABRIC TIP

This little quilt is a wonderful scrap project. 1/4-yd. quantities are listed since that is often the smallest cut a store will make, but you may find all the fabric you need in your scrap collection.

FIRST CUT			SECOND CUT	
Fabric and Yardage	Number of Pieces	Size	Number of Pieces	Size
BLOCK				
White Solid ½ yd	1	11″ × 12½″		
BORDER				
Black/White Check ¼ yd.	2	2½″ × 40″	2	2½″ × 11″
			2	2½″ × 12½″
CORNER SQUARES				
Black Print ¼ yd.	1	2½″ × 20″	4	2½″ square

Fabric and Yardage	Number of Pieces	Size/Shape
APPLIQUÉS[1]		
Blue/Black Stripe ¼ yd.	1	#1
Dk. Yellow Print ¼ yd.	1	#2
Med. Yellow Print ¼ yd.	1	#2$_R$
Lt. Yellow/Red Print ¼ yd.	2	#3
Med. Brown/ Yellow Print ¼ yd.	1	#4
Dk. Brown/ Yellow Print ¼ yd.	1	#4
Lt. Green Print ¼ yd.	1	#5
	1	#6
Dk. Green Print[2] ¼ yd.	2	⅞″ × 3½″ (Stems)

[1] Add ¼″ seam allowance to all appliqués except flower stems (bias strips).
[2] Cut strips for stems on the bias.
Note: Subscript $_R$ denotes reversed shape.

GREAT APPLIQUÉ TIP

Leaving seam allowance, cut out the center openings from the flower petals (#2, #2$_R$) and flower rings (#3). For reverse appliqué of each flower, turn under the edges of the openings, baste together the petals and ring, with the solid flower center (#4) behind them, then slipstitch around the openings. Arrange and appliqué the assembled flower in place on the quilt block.

LEAF EMBROIDERY DETAIL

STEM STITCH

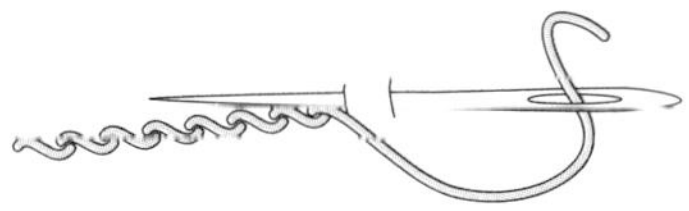

Quilt Center

1. Mark temporary guidelines for appliqué placement on quilt block, ½″ from top and bottom edges, and 1″ from sides.

2. Prepare fabric shapes for hand-appliqué.

3. Arrange and secure appliqués within guidelines on quilt block as shown; see the *Great Appliqué Tip* on page 53.

4. Hand-appliqué all shapes in place.

5. Embroider leaf stems with stem stitch, using matching floss; see stitch detail on page 53.

Border

Join corner squares to side border strips. Join border to quilt center, first plain strips at top and bottom, then pieced strips at sides.

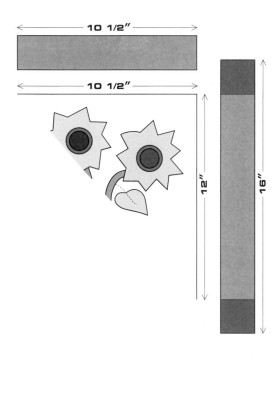

Echo quilting consists of concentric design lines stitched either inside or outside a patchwork shape, appliqué, or quilted motif. The quilting lines are spaced evenly, ¼" to ½" apart, to partially or completely fill a foreground or background.

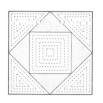 

Echoing inward is relatively straightforward: The lines repeat as far in toward the center of the shape as you desire. If smaller areas become defined by design lines meeting or merging, they too are marked for inward echoing.

Echoing outward can be a bit more challenging because, unless the background is the same shape as the design being echoed, new areas for filling will be defined not only by design lines but also by the outer edges. All of these newly defined areas can be quilted either outward or inward, depending on the effect you want.

Before beginning to mark your project for quilting, study it and decide on a route for the first line of stitches. Will the quilting go around individual shapes or around the general outline of the entire design? At the outer boundary of the background, will individual areas continue to echo outward with lines of stitching stopping at the edges, or will you treat the edges as design lines to be echoed inward? Do you want your project to have a random look, with different areas being treated in different ways (some echoing outward, some inward, some spiraling in toward the center, some boxed in)? Or do you want your design to radiate uniformly out from the center to fill the background smoothly? Also decide on the distance you want your design lines to be from the basic shape they echo and from each other.

1. Mark the first design line and notice any new, enclosed areas that appear.

2. Mark additional design lines outside the first one until only isolated areas remain unfilled.

3. Fill individual areas with design lines for either inward or outward echoing.

Marking the Quilting Designs

Mark design lines on quilt center for single-outline and echo quilting; see the *Great Marking Tip* on page 51 and *Planning Echo Quilting* on page 55.

◆ *For flower centers (#4)*: Mark a circle ¼" inside seam.

◆ *For pitcher handle*: Mark a line ¼" inside handle opening.

◆ *For remainder of quilt center*: Mark lines ¼" apart for outward echoing around pitcher (#1); flower petals (#2, #2$_R$) and flower stems; and leaf appliqués (#5, #6), extending design to fill background to block seam lines; do not mark lines on appliqués or embroidery.

Assembling the Quilt Layers

Prepare batting and backing. Assemble quilt layers.

Quilting the Designs

Quilt in-the-ditch around all appliqués and on interior seams of border strips. Quilt on all marked lines.

Trim batting and backing to ⅜" beyond outermost seam line. Bind quilt edges.

**ACTUAL-SIZE
PATTERNS**

(No seam allowance added)

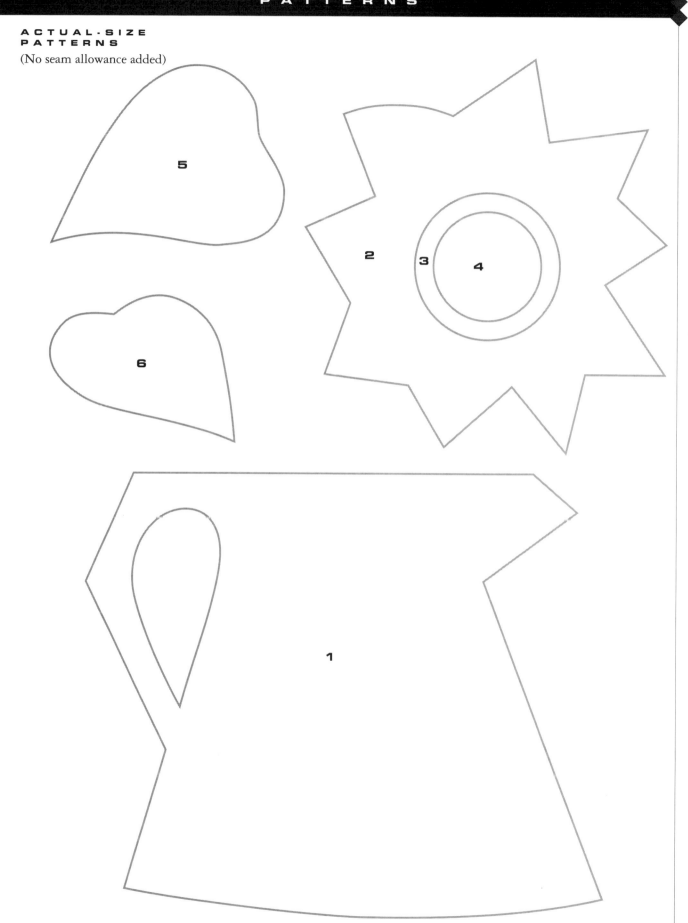

Something's Amiss-h

BY JUDY DOENIAS

J udy Doenias specializes in tessellated designs—those in which a few geometric shapes are arranged to form a pattern of offset, interlocking motifs. Clever use of color often makes the motifs shift, spin, or break away from one another. Here, pinwheel stars travel across a black ground. To emphasize the sense of their spinning through space, Judy quilted each with closely spaced concentric circles. The juxtaposition of basic geometric forms is a natural, yet somehow unexpected, choice.

GREAT PATTERN DRAFTING TIP

If you look carefully, you will see that the star is made from rectangles that are bisected diagonally (into two identical triangles) and turned at right angles to one another, then offset by a square that is equal to half the rectangular unit. The pinwheels appear when the adjacent diagonal halves of four rectangles are the same color. The pattern appears to break or shift when a black triangle is inserted.

Refer to this schematic to draft and then color your own version of this pattern.

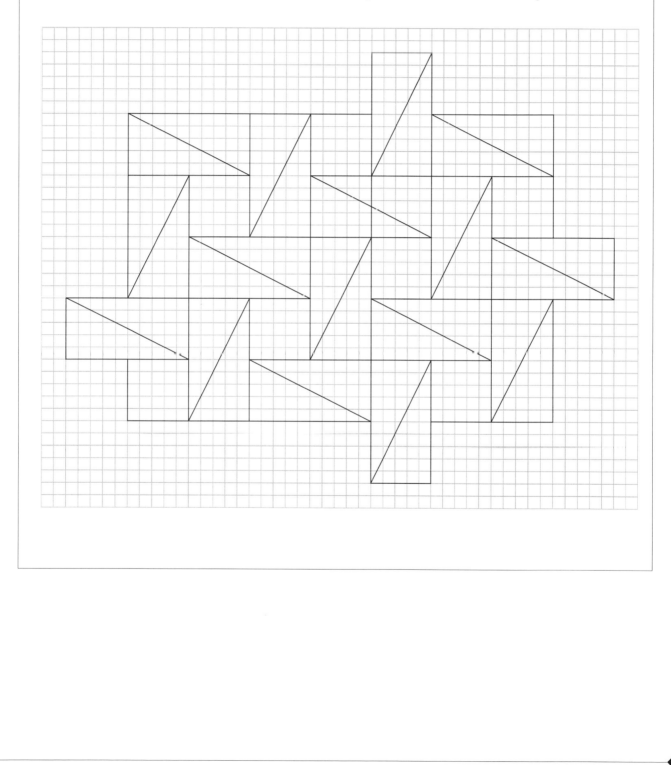

Creating the Quilting Designs

Judy used three designs to quilt this piece—for the stars, concentric circles; for the border, the star outline; and for the background, random short straight lines reminiscent of rainfall. Each design enhances the feeling of movement established by the patchwork. Judy marked the quilting patterns on the quilt top with a Berol Verithin silver pencil, which can be easily washed away when the stitching is complete. Adapt the following methods as appropriate to a quilt of your choice.

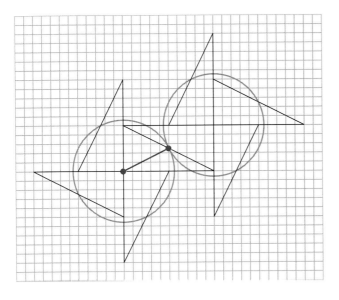

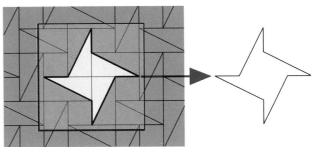

◆ *For the concentric circles:* Find the center of a star. Determine the radius of the largest circle you want (in this case, the radius is the distance between the two dots, which is half the length of the line diagonally bisecting the rectangles). Using a compass or circle template, mark this circle. Mark evenly spaced concentric circles within the first one as appropriate.

◆ *For the straight lines:* Use quilter's tape to establish a pattern of lines. For this quilt, they run along the bias and intersect randomly. You can place them in any direction and space them as you wish.

◆ *For the star outline:* Place transparent acetate over the pieced star motif (or motif you wish to use) and trace it. Cut it out and position it where desired on your quilt. For this quilt, Judy reduced the star and then rotated the template slightly each time she moved it, so the star spins along the border.

Quilted designs can be as beautiful when stitched on clothing as they are on home furnishings—indeed sashiko is traditionally used for garments. Here is a quick course in adapting quilting motifs to clothing:

- ◆ Unless you are an expert seamstress, choose garment patterns with minimal shaping so that the pieces can be flat while you are quilting them.
- ◆ Use a lightweight fabric such as China silk, wool challis or cotton for the top and lining layers, and flannel or another layer of the top fabric instead of batting.
- ◆ You may be able to quilt small areas such as collar or cuffs once the garment is assembled. Otherwise, cut out your garment and layer the individual pieces. Mark and quilt the designs as you would for any project.
- ◆ Sew the quilted pieces together, then finish the edges of the seam allowances neatly. Bind the hem and neck opening edges or turn them in toward the batting and slipstitch them closed, just as you would for a quilt.

Here are some suggestions for using the quilting motifs in this book to embellish clothing. Enlarge or reduce them with a photocopier if necessary. But don't stop with these—you can even adapt the motifs from the wholecloth doll quilt to embellish a wedding gown or evening coat.

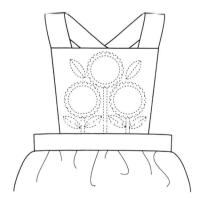

Make a muffler or stole. Quilt it with any of the sashiko motifs used on the kimono on pages 34 to 39.

Use Sonya Lee Barrington's hand-stippling technique to finish the collar and cuffs of an elegant blouse or jacket; see page 42.

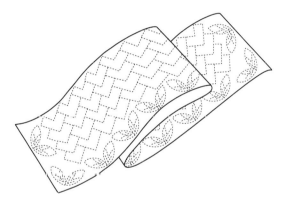

Use a cookie cutter motif to quilt the bib of child's pinafore or overalls; see page 19.

Use the grapevine motif from the wholecloth quilt on the front and back of a vest; see page 76.

Two Snail's Trail Quilts

BY DIANE RODE SCHNECK AND JUDY DOENIAS

W hen we searched for innovative quilting ideas, it was pure coincidence that two wonderful quilters showed us nontraditional finishes for the same classic pattern. Both responded to the spinning curves of the patchwork by quilting with contrasting curves. Diane, inspired by the movement in Vincent Van Gogh's Starry Night, drew free-form loopy curves randomly over her blue and black Night Quilt, then stitched them with royal blue and metallic threads. Judy developed a tour de force circular pattern; her technique follows.

Judy Doenias used a quilting design of swirling arcs and circles as a counterpoint to the angularity of the patchwork on her quilt. She drafted concentric circles, then photocopied and arranged them to form her design. She then traced the entire pattern onto lightweight nonwoven interfacing (available in sewing notions stores) that can be drawn on, basted in place, and quilted through, eliminating the need for marking the quilt.

After quilting, she carefully cut the interfacing away from the stitches with very sharp scissors and added another motif around the circular one, out to the edges of the quilt. The straight lines of this filler design were also quilted without marking: Judy used ordinary masking tape as guidelines, alternating widths of ½″ and 1″.

DESIGNER'S TIP

Judy recommends using a new roll of masking tape for quilting guidelines. Old tape gets soft and gooey and is more likely than new tape to leave a gunky residue on fabric. It's also a good idea to remove the tape from your quilt as soon as you're finished working on it each day.

Drafting the Circular Motif

To create her design, Judy first used a purchased quilting template of concentric circles to mark the larger circles of her motif, then she switched to a compass, marking successively smaller circles until the last one was about ½″ in diameter. The distance between pairs of circles on her template decreased proportionally in relation to the size of the circles (the distances vary from ⅝″ to ⅜″), so once she had set up the reversing arc-and-circle design she had more difficulty connecting and smoothing the intersecting curves than if the circles had been equidistant. We suggest you work this pattern out using equidistant circles.

For the smoothest curves with the least amount of hand-drawing, make your circular motif as directed below, using a compass or artist's circle templates. For a large motif, draft it at a reduced size (for example, one square on graph paper = 1″, or one square = ½″), then use a photocopier to enlarge the completed pattern to actual-size.

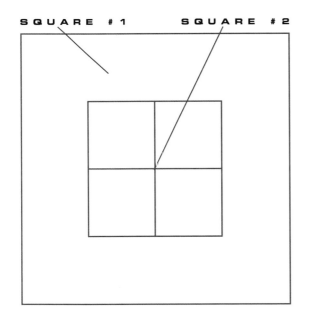

1. Mark straight lines (guidelines) on graph paper.
- Mark a square (Square #1), the same size as the design area of your quilt.
- Mark a smaller square (Square #2) centered in Square #1, with sides one-half the length of the sides of Square #1.
- Mark horizontal and vertical center lines on Square #2.

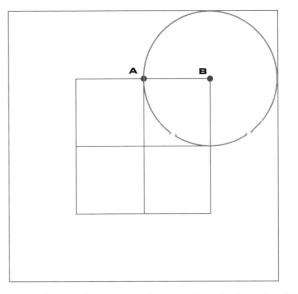

2. Mark a circle with a radius equal to the length of AB, with the center of the circle at B.

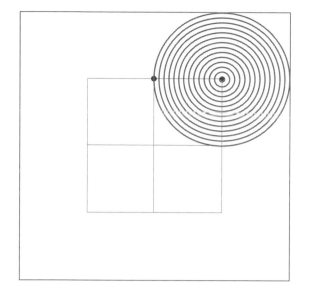

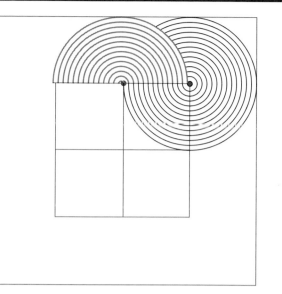

3. Mark smaller, concentric circles inside the first one, reducing the radius of each uniformly. (Plan your pattern so that after it is enlarged or reduced to fit your project, the distance between circles is between 1/4″ and 1/2″, and the smallest circle about 1/2″ in diameter.) Make 2 copies (or photocopies) of the circles and guidelines. Cut one copy of the circles in half. Retain one intact copy for Step 6.

4. Align the straight edge of one set of half-circles with the upper edge of Square #2. Slide it along the line until the largest arc on the half-circles meets the left side of the smallest complete circle; the center of the half-circles will be slightly to the left of A. Smooth out or regularize as necessary the joinings of all pairs of lines so that the arcs flow smoothly into the circles, then tape or glue the arcs in place.

5. Make and cut out 3 copies of the swirling arcs and circles from Step 4; trim them as close to the outermost lines as possible. Arrange the copies inside Square #1, aligning on the guidelines; overlap the arcs with the circles identically on all sides. Cut away the diamond-shaped center of the pattern.

6. Place the intact copy of complete circles from Step 3 behind the cutout; center it in all directions, then secure it in place.

7. Resize the pattern as desired, then trace the design lines, and Squares #1 and #2, onto nonwoven tracing material; only the curved lines (design lines) will be quilted.

Flaming Pinwheels

BY JOYCE SULLIVAN

Joyce Sullivan based this quilt on a pattern by Liz Porter, with whom she had taken a tessellation workshop. She quilted the black ground in red thread, using French curve rulers to create a wavelike pattern that crests gently between the sharply pointed blades of the pinwheels. See if you can figure out how this patchwork pattern differs from the one Judy Doenias used in Something's Amiss-h, and note how both quilters chose to balance the pronounced angles of their patchwork with curved quilting motifs.

Creating the Quilting Design

French curve templates are available in art supply and sewing notions stores. They come in a variety of shapes and sizes and are used to draw pleasing curves that are not circle-based. You can use part or all of one French curve to make a wave pattern, or combine several. Experiment on paper, reversing or overlapping the template shape to create a pattern that you like.

GREAT FRENCH CURVE TIP

You can use a French curve as you would any other template, marking its outline directly onto your fabric. To keep the pattern repeat consistent, establish some regular point of reference on your quilt top (for instance, the tip of every pinwheel blade). Then mark the French curve with tape to indicate where it should coincide with the reference point.

You can create a complex pattern repeat or motif by reversing or rotating your French curve, or by combining several curves, as Joyce did in the corners of her quilt. To mark such a pattern onto your quilt top consistently, draw it once on paper, and then make a new template of the complete pattern repeat.

A Tufted Quilt

This lovely scrap quilt is about a hundred years old. It is simply classic nine-patch blocks set on point with alternate plain squares. The quilt top is tufted, or tied, to the backing with cotton yarn and it has a homey, informal look. Note that there are nine ties on each plain block, placed to correspond to those on the pieced ones. The arrangement of the nine-patch blocks is random. The pattern is so familiar and easy to duplicate in any size, directions for the patchwork are not included here.

When to Tuft

Tufting requires minimal marking and is faster to stitch than fancier quilting, so one of the primary reasons to use it is to save time. Sometimes called tying, it is traditionally used on informal quilts, particularly those made from wool, and on quilts where the patchwork is an allover pattern of small pieces, with no plain areas to showcase elaborate stitching. Both log cabin and crazy quilts are good candidates for tufting. Tufting is also a good technique to choose if you are making a fluffy comforter, as it will not flatten the loft of a thick batting.

Where to Tuft

Tying can be done at strategic design points on the quilt top (corners or centers of blocks or strips, for example) or in an allover geometric design, such as a square grid, with no reference to the patchwork pattern. Ties are generally spaced 3″ to 6″ apart; although one at each block intersection should be sufficient with today's battings, which do not separate into lumps over time.

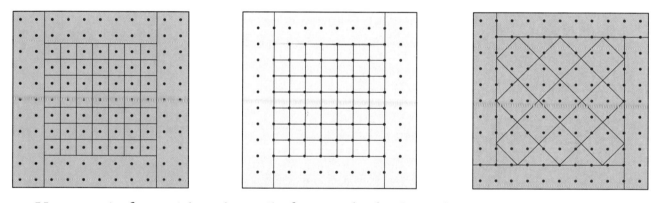

You can tie from either the quilt front or back, depending on whether or not you want the knots and thread ends to show. Likewise, you can tie with matching or contrasting thread or yarn which you can trim short or long as the piece requires. If you are making a wallhanging, consider adding strategically placed buttons or beads as you tie.

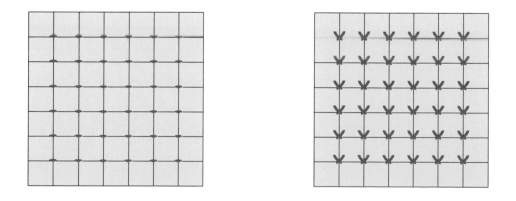

When choosing batting and thread for tufting, you must decide what effect you are trying to achieve. Do you want a fluffy quilt or one with a low loft? How apparent do you want the ties to be, should they blend or contrast with the fabrics? Is the quilt going on the bed or the wall? How often will it be laundered?

Batting

Because tufting is not dense like finely stitched quilting, it will not add stiffness to your quilt. To take advantage of this, choose batting with a soft hand, or drape, that is compatible with the weight of your quilt top. You can use batting that is either bonded or needle-punched. You can also use a flannel sheet or a blanket. If you are making a comforter, do not try to fill it with feathers or down, as the ties will not prevent them from drifting out of place.

Needles and Thread

Choose thread that complements the weight and style of your quilt, and that can be cleaned in the same manner. For lightweight fabrics you might use crochet cotton or fine cotton or linen yarn, or pearl cotton #5 or #8. You could even use very fine ribbon, or, for a small, elegant piece, buttonhole twist. For heavier fabrics, candlewick yarn or pearl cotton #3 works well; for wool, use baby or sportweight yarn.

Use an embroidery or crewel needle large enough to hold your thread, but no larger than necessary to pass easily through the layers, to prevent leaving noticeable holes in the fabric.

If your tufting design is based upon the intersection of patchwork pieces, you do not need to mark the quilt top. If not, you may be able to gauge the placement by eye or with a ruler as you work. Otherwise, mark the design on the quilt top first, then assemble, layer and baste the quilt layers in the same manner as for conventional quilting. Thread your needle with one or more 36″ lengths of thread.

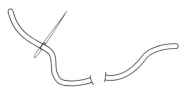

1. Make a single ¼″-long running stitch through all layers of the quilt at the location to be tufted, leaving a 3″ thread end.

2. Make a single backstitch through the same holes formed by the running stitch; do not cut the thread.

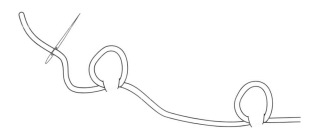

3. Make another running stitch and backstitch at the next and all subsequent locations to be tufted until the length of thread is used up.

4. Clip halfway between adjacent stitches and trim the ends if more than 3″. Tie each pair of thread ends in a square knot. Trim ends evenly to between ¼″ and 1″.

GREAT DESIGN IDEA

Use tufting to make a small wholecloth quilt for a pillow top, doll bed or wallhanging. Begin with solid fabric and tie it with contrasting thread; to create an interesting pattern, use several colors of thread and/or vary the spacing of the ties. To plan your design, tape tracing paper over graph paper, then plot the desired pattern with colored pencils. Here are some examples of patterns you could create working with an evenly spaced grid of ties.

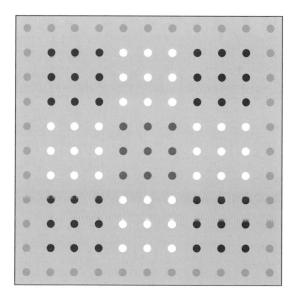

Wholecloth Doll Quilt

DESIGNED BY MIMI SHIMMIN
QUILTED BY MARY LEAHY

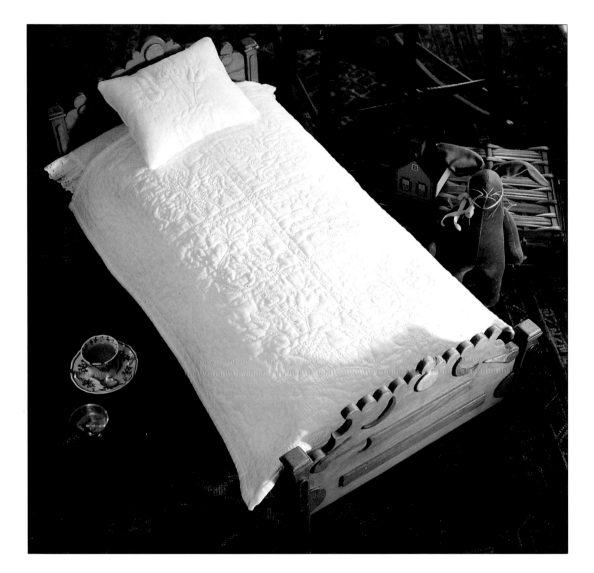

What quilter does not aspire to someday stitching a spectacular white-on-white quilt? Here is one small enough to complete in a busy lifetime. The patterns can be resized with a photocopier if you wish, worked together as a wholecloth quilt, or used individually to quilt blocks, sashing or borders wherever you like. We used trapunto to add extra relief to the doll quilt; turn to page 80 to see the effect when contrasting thread or pearl cotton is used.

Note: In the following directions the components are defined by lines of quilting rather than by seams. Dimensions for the quilt top are finished size.

QUILT TOP
One rectangle,
20¾″ × 27¼″

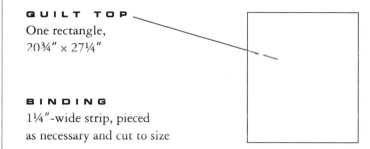

BINDING
1¼″-wide strip, pieced
as necessary and cut to size

FABRIC AND CUTTING LIST

Yardages are based on 44″ fabric; see the *Great Fabric Tip* on page 79. Cut rectangles following chart; see *Using the Cutting Charts*, page 88. Cut binding as directed below. All dimensions include ¼″ seam allowance and binding includes extra length.

DIMENSIONS

FINISHED QUILT
20¾″ × 27¼″

MATERIALS

☐ **WHITE SOLID**
2 yds. tightly woven fabric
(for quilt top, backing* and
binding)

☐ **WHITE SOLID**
¾ yd. loosely woven fabric
(for lining trapunto)

BINDING
Use ¼ yd. tightly woven white
solid to cut and piece a 1¼″ ×
110″ strip.

BATTING*

THREAD
Sewing, quilting, embroidery

YARN/CORD
Cotton yarn/cord, ⅛″ diameter

**POLYESTER
FIBERFILL**
Loose fiberfill, for trapunto

*Backing and batting should be cut and
pieced as necessary so they are at least 4″
larger than quilt top on all sides, then
trimmed to size after quilting.

Fabric and Yardage	Number of Pieces			Size
	For Quilt Top	For Backing	For Lining	
White Solid (tightly woven) 1¾ yd.	1	—	—	21¼″ × 27¾″
	—	1	—	29″ × 36″ (includes extra length and width)
White Solid (loosely woven) ¾ yd.	—	—	1	21¼″ × 27¾″

Marking the Quilting Designs

On this project the seams between components (blocks, sashing, and borders) are simulated by straight lines of quilting around individual quilting designs. Each round dot on patterns and diagrams represents a French knot, which is embroidered after trapunto and conventional quilting are complete.

Mark design lines on quilt top as directed below. Use actual-size motif patterns on pages 82 to 87; do not re mark straight outlines, which are given for positioning only.

1. Mark outer edge of second border ⅜" inside seam line of quilt top, outlining a 20½" × 27" design area, centered. (Subsequent diagrams do not show fabric that extends beyond this design area.)

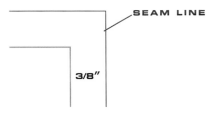

2. Mark additional outlines for blocks, sashing strips, and two borders as shown.

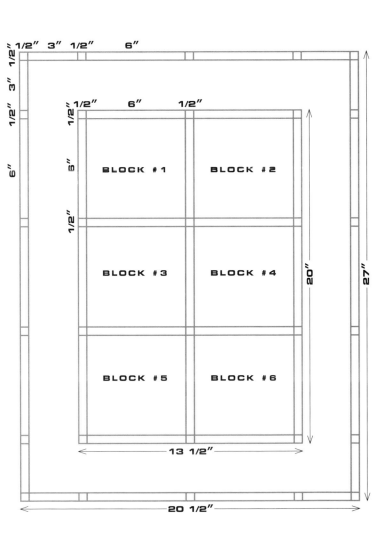

3. Mark floral motif on each block.

- *For Block #1:* Mark half-pattern on left half of block, centered between top and bottom edges; do not mark diamond grid on center flower yet. Reverse pattern to mark right half of block, then mark diamond grid on center flower.
- *For Blocks #2, #3, #4, and #5:* Mark pattern on each block, centered.
- *For Block #6:* Mark half-pattern on right half of block, centered between top and bottom edges. Reverse pattern to mark left half of block.

BLOCK #1

BLOCK #2

BLOCK #3

BLOCK #4

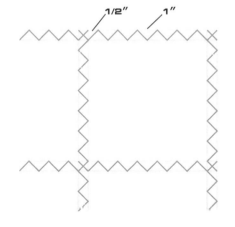

BLOCK #5

BLOCK #6

4. Mark geometric designs on sashing.

- *For sashing strips:* Mark a zigzag of 1"-long triangles on each strip.
- *For sashing squares:* Connect corners of each square to mark an ✕.

1/2"   1"

5. Mark motifs on first border, rotating quilt to mark each border side.

- *For each corner:* Mark heart and leaf at lower right, aligning center of heart with 45° diagonal center of corner. Reverse pattern, aligning on heart, to mark second leaf.
- *For each long side:* Mark grape cluster, centered between leaves and between inner and outer border edges.

6. Mark geometric designs on second border.

- Mark strips with zigzags of 1″-long triangles and border squares with ✗'s in same manner as for sashing.

Trapunto

If you wish, add a trapunto relief to the quilt at this time; see *Working Trapunto,* opposite. Baste lining to back of quilt top. Hand-quilt motifs on blocks and first border that will be stuffed/corded for high relief; do not stitch single lines, such as small stems, tendrils, and zigzag grids, which will be quilted through a layer of batting in the traditional manner after stuffing. Stuff/cord the trapunto design areas.

In trapunto, parts of the quilting motifs are stuffed or corded to create high-relief designs. A loosely woven lining is placed behind the quilt top, with no batting between. Small closed areas of the motifs, such as leaves, stems, flower petals or the rim of a basket are outlined with quilting stitches and then filled with lengths of cotton yarn/cord and/or loose fiberfill that are inserted through the lining.

Preparing Quilt Top and Lining

1. Mark trapunto and traditional quilting designs on quilt top.
- *For stuffed designs:* Mark a single, closed outline for each shape to be stuffed.
- *For corded designs:* Mark double outlines to form channels slightly wider than diameter of yarn to be used, maintaining a uniform distance between pairs of parallel lines.

2. Cut lining same size as quilt top.
3. Pin lining to wrong side of quilt top, aligning edges; baste together as for traditional quilting but with 6" to 8" between columns and rows of basting stitches. Do not baste over trapunto designs. Machine-stitch ¼" from edges.
4. Quilt by hand or machine on trapunto design lines.

Stuffing

1. Use appliqué scissors carefully to make a slit in lining at center of shape to be stuffed.

2. Working through slit, insert loose bits of fiberfill between quilt top and lining, using a blunt tool such as a crochet hook to distribute stuffing evenly.

3. Fill shape lightly but completely, checking front of quilt often. Do not overstuff.
4. Close slit with loose cross stitches or whipstitches.

Cording

1. Thread a long, blunt rug or tapestry needle with 15" to 18" length of yarn/cord.
2. Working through lining only, use tip of needle to make hole in channel large enough for needle to slip through.
3. Insert needle and slide it through channel between fabric layers as far as it can reach, then bring it out again on lining side. Pull cord until end disappears into needle entry point.

4. Reinsert needle at exit point and work it further along channel, then bring it up and re-enter channel as needed to cord its entire length.
- *To end a length of cord:* Bring needle out through lining and clip cord close to fabric, massaging the last needle exit point until end of cord disappears inside it.
- *To start a new length of cord:* Overlap end of previous length at least ½" to prevent gaps in corded outline.

Prepare batting and backing. Assemble quilt layers. Hand-quilt on all marked lines not previously stitched, except round dots.

Embroidery

Use 2 or 3 strands of embroidery floss to stitch a French knot at each marked round dot on quilt top.

Finishing the Quilt

Trim batting and backing even with quilt top and lining. Bind quilt edges.

GREAT FABRIC TIP

Although Mimi Shimmin chose white fabric for her quilt, you could make yours in any solid color. If you want to make a light color quilt top, use matching or white fabric for both the backing and lining; darker colors might show through as shadowing on the front.

To keep white or pale fabric from getting dirty while work is in progress, be sure your hands, work space, and tools are spotlessly clean and grease-free.

To avoid putting marks on your quilt, you can transfer the pattern for the quilting designs to tear-away interfacing or mark straight quilting lines with tape; see the Tips on pages 51 and 63.

Instead of leaving your project out in the open when it isn't being worked on, place it folded (inside out) or flat into a pillowcase.

GREAT DESIGN IDEA

You can make a small pillow to go with the doll quilt by centering and quilting one of the block motifs on a piece of matching fabric. The pillow in the photo is about 10" wide and 7" high and is finished with a plain knife edge. It is stuffed with fiberfill, but you could fill yours with balsam or potpourri instead.

Wholecloth Pillows

Mimi Shimmin designed the Wholecloth Doll Quilt so that the motifs could be recombined to make other projects. The sashing and border motifs are proportioned so that they can be wrapped around a single block motif, or extended to fit around a layout that has any number of blocks.

We made two pillows using the motifs from the middle blocks of the doll quilt. Each has the zigzag sashing and outer border along with part of the heart and leaf inner border. The lavender pillow is quilted with a slightly darker lavender thread, the white pillow with pretty shades of pearl cotton #8. Because the designs are more visible with the contrasting stitching, neither was worked with trapunto.

Cut a 16½" square of fabric for each pillow top and back. Make or purchase complementary cording; you will need about 2 yards.

Marking the Quilting Designs

Refer to the directions for the doll quilt to mark the designs on the pillow top.

1. Select one of the block motifs from the doll quilt. Center and mark it on the pillow top. Mark zigzag sashing and a matching outer border all around it.

2. Use the corner pattern on page 82 to mark a heart in each corner and one leaf on each side of the inner border.

Quilting

Layer pillow top, batting and lining. Quilt with thread to match your fabric, or use one or more contrasting colors of thread for a less formal look. Add French knots.

Finishing

After the quilting and embroidery are complete, add cording and a pillow back and insert a 16"-square knife-edge pillow form.

ACTUAL-SIZE
PATTERNS

LONG BORDER SIDE

BORDER
CORNER

B L O C K   # 1

B L O C K   # 6

BLOCK #2

BLOCK #3

BLOCK #4

BLOCK #5

Appendix

The sample cutting charts and schematics below demonstrate how these elements work together to provide the information needed to cut most of the pieces for any quilt project in the Better Homes and Gardens® Creative Quilting Collection volumes. Any additional cuts, such as for binding, can be found in the Fabric and Cutting List for each project.

DRAFTING SCHEMATIC —————————
Drafting schematics, which do not include seam allowance, are provided for your convenience as an aid in preparing templates.

DRAFTING SCHEMATIC
(No seam allowance added)

CUTTING SCHEMATIC —————————
Cutting schematics, which do include seam allowance, can be used for preparing templates (with seam allowance included) but are given primarily as an aid for speed-cutting shapes using a rotary cutter and special rulers with angles marked on them.

CUTTING SCHEMATICS
(Seam allowance included)

 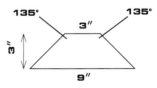

FABRIC AND YARDAGE
This column gives the color and amount of fabric needed to cut groups of shapes, rounded up to the next ¼ yard. To change the color scheme of a project, refer to the dimensions given for individual groups of shapes and use (combine them as needed) to calculate the new yardage.

FIRST CUT
Cut the number of pieces in the sizes indicated on either the lengthwise or crosswise grain unless otherwise stated, using templates or rotary cutting rulers. For 40"-long strips, cutting completely across the width of the fabric usually provides the most economical cuts.

SECOND CUT
Cut the number of pieces in the sizes and/or shapes indicated, referring to the cutting schematics for angles and cut sizes. Reversed pieces are designated by a subscript $_R$ (e.g., the reverse of a B patch is designated B_R) and can frequently be obtained from the same strips as their mirror images by cutting the two shapes alternately.

BORDER
From ½ yd. blue check cut two 2½" × 29" and two 2½" × 32" border strips.

FOOTNOTE
Use the cited instructions for Speedy Triangle Squares and mark the grids in the layout indicated.

APPLIQUÉS
From ¼ yd. red floral cut 16 flowers and 8 buds. From ¼ yd. blue floral cut 56 leaves. Reversed pieces are designated by a subscript $_R$ and these patterns should be turned over before marking onto fabric.

8 RED SOLID A'S
From ¼ yd. red solid, cut one 3⅞" × 20" strip. From strip cut four 3⅞" squares. Cut squares in half to make 8 right-triangle A's.

6 WHITE SOLID C'S
From ¼ yd. white solid cut one 3½" × 40" strip. From strip cut six trapezoids.

FOOTNOTE REFERENCE
See the footnote underneath the chart for additional information about cutting this group of shapes.

FIRST CUT			SECOND CUT	
Fabric and Yardage	Number of Pieces	Size	Number of Pieces	Shape
PLAIN PATCHES				
Red Solid ¼ yd.	1	3⅞" × 20"	8	A
	1	3½" × 40"	8	B
White Solid ¼ yd.	1	3⅞" × 20"	8	A
	1	3½" × 40"	6	C
SPEEDY TRIANGLE SQUARES				
Red Solid and White Solid ½ yd. each	2	16½" × 20⅜"	72	B/B[1]
BORDER				
Blue Check ½ yd.	2	2½" × 29"		
	2	2½" × 32"		

[1]See *Speedy Triangle Squares* (page 00). Mark 4 × 5 grids with 3⅞" squares.

APPLIQUÉS		
Fabric and Yardage	Number of Pieces	Shape
Red Floral ¼ yd.	16	Flower
	8	Bud
Blue Floral ¼ yd.	56	Leaf

Refer as well to Great Quiltmaking: All the Basics, *the detailed companion to the volumes in the* Better Homes and Gardens® Creative Quilting Collection.

Assembling the Layers

Layer and baste the quilt on a large, flat work surface, such as a dining table, countertop, or floor. Having a helper for assembling and basting the quilt can make both processes faster and more enjoyable.

LAYERING

1. Place quilt backing wrong side up on work surface. If you are using a free-standing work surface, such as a table or island counter, which is smaller than the backing, center fabric on top so that equal lengths of fabric hang down on each side, like a tablecloth.

2. Position batting on top of backing, aligning edges. Baste batting and backing together with a single large cross-stitch in the center.

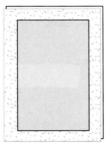

3. Center quilt top on batting, right side up.

BASTING

Hold the quilt layers together with straight pins, then baste with either thread or safety pins as follows:

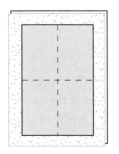

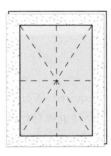

1. Baste along horizontal and vertical centers of quilt first, then diagonally in both directions.
- *For thread-basting:* Make stitches about 2″ long and 3″ to 4″ apart.
- *For safety-pin basting:* Space pins 3″ to 4″ apart.

2. Make additional horizontal and vertical lines of basting 3″ to 4″ apart (or follow batting manufacturer's directions for spacing).
- *For quilting to be stitched in a hoop:* Use thread for basting, and make stitches shorter (1″ to 2″ long) and more closely spaced (1″ to 2″ apart) because the hoop will be repeatedly moved and repositioned.

Hand-Quilting

If you will be quilting in a frame, secure the long edges of the backing to the long parallel bars of the frame, following the frame manufacturer's directions, and rotate the frame bars during quilting to reach all areas of design.

If you will be working with the quilt in your lap (with or without a hoop), the edges should be temporarily finished, by basting the backing as self-binding; see page 94, to protect them during the quilting process. (NOTE: If you use a hoop, retighten and reposition it as needed to stitch all areas of design.)

Quilting stitches (running stitch or stab stitch) should be small (6 to 12 per inch), and even, so they look the same on the back of the quilt as they do on the front.

STITCHING

♦ To plan as continuous a stitching path as possible, examine each different design before quilting. When a path is interrupted, you can create a tiny bridge of stitches to connect lines of design, run the needle through the batting to a new location, or end the thread and begin a new one.

♦ Plan the most continuous path for your quilting to avoid as much as possible either retracing an already stitched line or breaking the thread to begin stitching a new line.

TO PLAN A QUILTING ROUTE

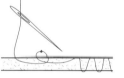

TO BEGIN A LENGTH OF THREAD:
Knot one end of the thread. Insert the needle into the quilt back and batting about 1″ from where you want to make the first stitch. Bring it out on the quilt top where the first stitch will be. Give the thread a tug to pull the knot up through the quilt back and embed it in the batting.

TO END A LENGTH OF THREAD:
Make a small knot in the thread a scant ¼″ above the quilt back. Make a tiny backstitch and run the needle forward through the batting and bring it out on the quilt back about 1″ away. Pull the thread taut and clip it, releasing the end to snap back into the batting.

RUNNING STITCH
Only one thimble is required. Working from the top of the quilt, load the needle with as many stitches at one time as possible and pull the needle out with your upper hand.

STAB STITCH
Two thimbles are required. Working from both sides of the quilt, push the needle through the quilt with one hand and pull it out again with the other hand. Pull the thread completely through the quilt each time the needle exits the quilt.

Machine-Quilting

If you are machine-quilting a large project, the quilt should be rolled and folded before it is fed through the machine to make it easier to handle. It may be necessary to reroll and refold the quilt before each new area is stitched.

You can also place a table in front of the sewing machine to support the weight of the quilt as the machine moves it forward, instead of letting the quilt drop to the floor, which can create drag.

Use a quilting foot or even-feed walking foot for machine-quilting. Adjust the stitch length for 6 to 12 stitches per inch, and loosen the upper tension if you use invisible thread. Just as for hand-quilting, machine-quilting should be done from the center of the quilt outward in all directions.

To begin and end a line of stitching, either make a few tiny backstitches and clip the threads close to the quilt top, or knot and embed long thread ends in the batting in the same manner as for finishing hand-quilting threads.

Separate Bindings

Following are several methods for applying a binding to an assembled quilt. You can cut the binding strips on either the straight or bias grainline of your fabric.

CUTTING BIAS STRIPS

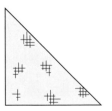

1. Cut a fabric square in half diagonally (along the bias).

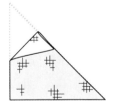

2. Beginning at one 45° corner, fold fabric repeatedly, aligning bias edges.

3. Cut strips parallel to bias edge.
4. Join strip ends to make a longer strip.

SIMPLE CONTINUOUS BINDING

1. Press under seam allowance on one long edge and one end of binding strip.

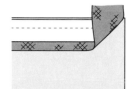 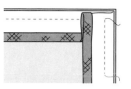  

2. Pin and stitch binding strip to quilt top, aligning seam lines, beginning at center of one quilt edge with folded end of strip and stopping at seam line of next quilt edge; break threads.

3. To miter corner, press strip away from quilt on a 45° angle, then press it back over quilt. Stitch, beginning at end of previous stitching line (a tuck will form at corner). At beginning point, trim binding and lap ends 1"; stitch.

4. Fold binding over corners to backing, forming miters at tucks. Position long folded edge of binding over seam line, forming miters at corners. Slipstitch, stitching into miters to secure.

INDIVIDUAL BINDING STRIPS

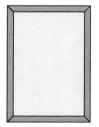 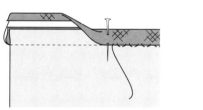 

1. Prepare simple binding.

◆ *For mitered corners:* Stitch binding strips to quilt top, making machine-stitched mitered corners. Fold binding over quilt edges to backing; pin, making neat mitered or butted corners.

◆ *For butted corners:* Stitch one pair of binding strips to opposite edges of quilt top. Trim ends even with quilt. Fold strips to backing; slipstitch. Apply second pair of strips to remaining quilt edges in same manner, folding ends under instead of trimming.

Binding strip length = Length of quilt edge + 1"

FRENCH FOLD BINDING

◆ French fold binding is made the same way as other separate, continuous bindings but uses more fabric because it is applied doubled.

Binding strip width = (Binding width x 4) + ½"
Binding strip length = Perimeter of quilt + 1"

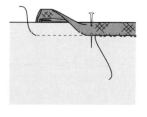

1. Press under ¼" at one end of binding strip. Press strip in half lengthwise, right side out.

2. Apply folded binding as for other bindings: Place raw edges of binding toward raw edge of quilt. It will not be necessary to press under free edge of binding as it is already folded.

Backing As Self-Binding

Baste the quilt layers together along the outer seam line. Place the quilt flat, right side up, and bind the quilt, making mitered or butted corners. (NOTE: Directions are given below for using the backing as the binding, but the quilt top can be used instead, if desired.)

Batting width beyond seam line = Binding width

Backing width beyond seam line = (Binding width x 2) + ½″

MITERED CORNERS

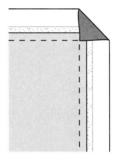 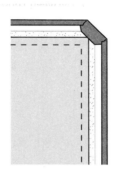 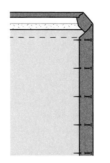 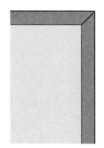

1. Press one corner of backing over quilt top, so that tip meets corner of seam line.

2. Trim away tip of corner. Press backing edges ¼″ to front.

3. Fold one edge over quilt top, covering seam line.

4. Fold adjoining edge, forming mitered corner. Slipstitch.

BUTTED CORNERS

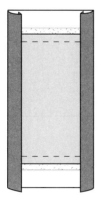

1. Press one pair of opposite backing edges ¼″ to front. Fold backing to front again, covering seam line; pin.

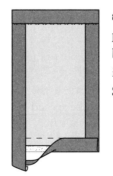

2. Press and pin remaining backing edges in same manner. Slipstitch.

Hanging a Quilt with Rings

Lightweight plastic rings (available in crafts shops and hardware stores) provide a simple way to hang a quilt. For a small wallhanging (up to about 20″ square), three ½″diameter rings should be sufficient. For a larger project, buy enough rings so that they can be spaced 7″ to 9″ apart along the top edge of the quilt. You will need to affix one small nail (or picture hook) in the wall to support each plastic ring.

1. Position one ring on backing, centered and 1″ below top edge. Sew center bottom of ring in place securely with a few hand-stitches, making sure stitches don't show through on front of quilt.

2. Stitch a ring to each end of backing top, 1″ from top and side edges.

3. Space any additional rings evenly between those already stitched in place.

4. To mount quilt, place rings over nails (or picture hooks) on wall.

Hanging a Quilt with a Sleeve

A fabric sleeve can be sewn to the quilt backing for holding a wooden dowel or lattice strip that will support the weight of the quilt evenly and completely across the top. The larger and heavier the quilt, the sturdier the dowel or lattice strip must be.

The ends of the dowel or lattice strip can extend beyond the quilt sides and be capped with decorative finials, or they can stop just short of the sides and support the quilt invisibly.

Dowels can be supported with appropriate sizes of finishing (headless) nails, cup hooks, or small brackets. If using nails, be sure they extend sufficiently from the wall to hold the dowel.

MAKING A SLEEVE

1. Cut a 3″-wide fabric strip 2½″ shorter than width of quilt. (NOTE: If the quilt is very wide or heavy, make several shorter sleeves that will be spaced evenly across the quilt so the dowel can be affixed to supporting nails in several places.)

2. Press under ¼″ on each edge of strip. Topstitch fold allowance at ends.

3. Center strip (sleeve) across quilt backing ½″ below top edge; pin.

4. Hand-stitch long edges of sleeve securely to quilt backing, making sure stitches don't show through on front of quilt. Do not stitch ends.

1. Cut dowel (or lattice strip) 1″ shorter than quilt width. If supporting with nails, drill a small hole ¼″ in from each end.

2. Seal wood with polyurethane to prevent wood seepage from discoloring fabric. Let dry thoroughly. (NOTE: Follow manufacturer's directions for method of application and drying time.)

◆ *If using nails to support quilt:* Measure, mark, and affix them to wall the same distance apart as holes in wood.

◆ *If using brackets or cup hooks to support quilt:* Measure, mark, and affix to wall appropriately.

3. Slide dowel (or lattice strip) through fabric sleeve, centering it between quilt sides so that holes in wood are at ends of sleeve.

4. To mount quilt, line up holes in wood with nails in wall. Press dowel in place, making sure nails go into holes.

Hook-and-Loop Tape

Hook-and-loop tape (such as Velcro) provides another simple method for hanging a quilt and still allowing for it to be cleaned or laundered, because the tape is washable.

HOOK STRIP ON BACKING

LOOP STRIP ON LATTICE

1. Cut a 2″-wide strip of hook-and-loop tape 2″ shorter than quilt width.

2. Cut a 2″-wide wooden lattice strip same length as tape. Seal wood and let dry in same manner as for sleeves, above.

3. Separate the tape halves so that you have one strip with hooks (stiffer strip) and one with loops (softer strip).

4. Center the hook strip across quilt backing ½″ below top edge. Hand-sew all strip edges securely in place, making sure stitches don't show through on front of quilt.

5. Attach the loop strip to lattice, aligning edges, using a staple gun or hot glue gun.

6. Measure, mark, and affix lattice securely to wall with nails, with loop strip facing out. Place nails ½″ from lattice ends and in the center. Add nails between those already placed, dividing and subdividing spaces, using as many nails as needed to support weight of quilt.

7. To mount quilt, align hook and loop halves of tape. Press tape halves together firmly.